Contents

Chapter 1

Man Comes to Ulster

It is interesting to speculate who the first Ulstermen were and where in the north they first settled, but it is very difficult to answer these questions. One has to leap forward to the seventeenth century to find some information about what happened in prehistory, for the seventeenth century saw the breakdown of Gaelic society as the English started to settle in the province. During the eighteenth century, Michael O'Clearly and his assistants laboured in Donegal to provide a history of Ireland from the earliest times to the seventeenth century. This account is known as *The Annals of the Kingdom of Ireland* or, more commonly, *The Annals of the Four Masters*. According to Michael O'Clearly's findings, man first came to Ireland in about 1700 BC in the person of the Tuatha Dé Danann, who had been driven underground. In *The Annals of the Four Masters* one learns that Ireland had been colonized on a number of earlier occasions by various tribes, and that the first person to step on Irish soil was one Cossair, a grandfather of Noah, about 2,242 years after the Creation (and forty days before the Flood). Geoffrey Keating, also writing in the seventeenth century, reveals that the territory of Ulster was first set out as a province by the Fir Bolg. *The Annals of the Four Masters* describes them as ruling Ireland about 1900 BC. The first ruler of Ulster was Rudraighe (Rory).

The Ulster planters might have accepted this information as fact.

Like Keating and the medieval annalists they were faced with the same difficulty when it came to obtaining information about people in Ulster and the rest of Ireland before the Flood.

In the twenty-first century we realize that it is not useful to rely on old books to tell us what happened in Ulster in prehistoric times. Some of the stories had originally been copied down on stones. The written accounts give no accurate facts about the development of Ulster before the arrival of St Patrick in the fifth century. Knowledge of the prehistoric period comes from archaeology – the reconstruction of the past through the study of objects, settlements, burials and other phenomena. These do not provide us with precise dates like those that were taken for granted by historians in the seventeenth century. Their date for the arrival of man in Ireland is at least 4,000 years off the mark. According to the seventeenth-century myth, the colonization of Ulster took place about 7000 BC, but there is no evidence for this. The date is 3,000 years before the invention of writing anywhere in the world.

The radiocarbon that is found in the atmosphere is present in all organic matter. On the death of any living creature, radiocarbon starts to disintegrate at a known rate. Measurement of the amount of residual radiocarbon in substances, such as a wood ash from a prehistoric hearth, provides us with the date when the tree died. From this evidence we know that man has been in Ulster for at least 9,000 years.

Most of the northern parts of Europe experienced long periods of intense cold, called the Ice Ages, and these occurred during the Pleistocene epoch. During the Ice Ages, Ireland, like most of Northern Europe (and much of North America), was covered in extensive ice. Even during warmer periods, the Irish landscape was still very cold – much like Siberia today. When Ulster was covered in ice, possibly up to 350 metres thick, this was enough to prevent settlers from casting down roots. However, during the warmer periods the lands would have supported mammoths, reindeer and wild horses – animals that were hunted elsewhere on the Continent at that time. Remains of mammoths which lived over 40,000 years ago have been discovered near Crumlin, County Antrim. It is probably easier for people to live in the conditions found during the Pleistocene epoch than we might at first think. In colder periods the waters of the world's great oceans were locked up in the great glaciers. The level of the sea dropped between Britain and Europe and between Ireland and Britain. Here the seabed is only 90 metres below the surface, so during the Pleistocene epoch it may have been possible to walk from France or Holland across to Britain. At any rate, man had been travelling between Europe and Britain for many thousands of years.

The Pleistocene epoch is commonly known as the Old Stone Age. This was the age of the world's great game-hunters, and survival was based on pursuing herds of mammoths, horses, cattle and reindeer across the open grasslands. However, there is no solid evidence of such hunt-based societies existing in Eastern Ireland or Scotland. A number of Ulster antiquarians of the late nineteenth and early twentieth centuries believed they had found traces of Palaeolithic man in Ulster. Mammoth teeth and bones have been found both along the Antrim coast, from Larne to Glenariff, and in County Cavan, but there is not much evidence that they were hunted by man. Stone dwellings from many sites along the Antrim coast were at one time thought to derive from glacial times, but it soon became clear that they dated from only 7,000 years ago or less. Conditions in Ulster were such that hunters were not tempted to cross over until long after the end of the glacial period. On the other hand, some archaeologists believe that men were hunting in Ulster before this, although their remains have not been found. Simple flints found in graves near Drogheda appear to be similar to those produced by man in Southern Britain several hundred thousand years ago.

The evidence suggests that man eventually settled in Ireland during the Palaeolithic epoch, and it is most likely that their first settlements were in Ulster, but the ice sheets have scoured away evidence of any already existing settlements. It is possible that evidence for Palaeolithic peoples will eventually be discovered in the south of the Blackwater Valley in the province of Munster, which lay beyond the ice sheets of the previous glaciation. We believe that man settled in Ulster about 9,000 years ago.

By about 1200 BC the climate had become warm enough for the ice sheets to melt. Trees spread north from Southern Europe into

Britain and Ireland. The sea was still shallow between Ireland and Britain and the Continent. The first trees to emerge in the new landscape were junipers and willow, which are tolerant to cold and which can survive on very poor soils. After the last ice age the terrain of Ulster was largely gravel, until trees and other plants could establish themselves and begin the process of soil formation by adding the organic matter that makes the earth fertile. Following the arrival of willow and juniper trees, there was another cold period, but with the return of warmer conditions birch and hazel forests were established. The colonization of Ulster by trees and other plants permitted the coming of animals that could not have survived on the ice sheets.

The level of the earth's seas rose, until, by the third millennium BC, Ireland became separated from mainland Britain. The Irish Sea was now a barrier to settlement in Ireland. This helps us to explain why the variety of flora and fauna is not so great as on the mainland. The absence of snakes in Ireland, later attributed to St Patrick, is a well-known example. There were thirty-two species of mammoth native to Britain, but only ten of them were found in Ireland.

Changing conditions gave rise to a dramatic change in Ireland's landscape. After the Pleistocene epoch ended there were no great expanses of grassland and the great animals that perhaps roamed the east and north of Ulster became extinct. Their place was taken in Europe by reindeer, red deer, elk, and aurochs (great wild cattle). Also present were the smaller roe deer and wild pig. Of these animals only the red deer was a feature of Ulster. Fish and shellfish played a leading role in Stone Age man's diet in the province, and new weapons and tools were made to help primitive man to hunt these animals. These new stone tools are known as microliths, and they became increasingly sophisticated as the Palaeolithic (Old Stone Age) gave way to the Mesolithic (New Stone Age).

In Britain the early colonists stuck together in bands made up of several families. They usually moved about, following the seasonal migration of animals like the red deer or pursuing fish, such as salmon, in their annual run up rivers. The sites of Mesolithic camps have been discovered in Scotland and Ireland, and in England and Wales there are also a large number of settlements.

8

Like hunter-gatherers today, the Mesolithic peoples would have used tools and containers of wood, plants and animal skins. These have long ago disintegrated and no trace of them remains. Soils in Ulster are often acidic, which speeds up the disintegration process. However, stone tools, such as flakes of flint, have been discovered by archaeologists and amateur collectors in newly ploughed fields or along riverbanks.

It is useful for us to complete this survey of the earlier Mesolithic period in Ireland by examining a map of sites where evidence of dwellers in the island has been found.

At a glance it is seen that the great majority of them are situated in Ulster, especially in counties Antrim and Down – the eastern counties. There are only a few sites on the Leinster coast. This suggests that the first colonists lived in Ulster rather than elsewhere in Ireland. The earliest settlers seem to have come from Britain to Antrim and Down, but can we be sure of this? At most of the sites, flint tools have been found; where, then, did the flints originate?

About 1 million years ago, Ireland lay under the sea. On the bottom of the sea, deep layers of chalk accumulated, and in the chalk nodules of flint are found. This phenomenon can be seen near the beaches of Glenarm and Ballycastle. Chalk layers about 100 metres thick covered Ireland at one time, but they are now confined to North-East Ulster. Here molten rock pushed through the chalk about 65 million to 50 million years ago and covered it with basalt. Whereas much of the chalk that covered Ulster has been preserved, the chalk that covered most of the rest of Ireland has been eroded away over millions of years. Flint therefore is limited to North-East Ulster, except for what was scattered over the countryside by movements of the ice sheets. It is interesting to speculate that the earliest colonists in Ireland lived only in areas where there was a supply of flint, as flint tools were essential to their way of life. Maybe the first colonists to arrive in Ulster came looking for flints. Later, however, competition for food may have encouraged migration into other parts of the island, where different stones were used to make tools. In the province of Munster and Connaught very good tools made of chert and rhyolite have been found at Mesolithic sites; they have also been found in smaller quantities in other parts of Ireland.

The majority of sites have been discovered by amateurs, notably by members of the Belfast Natural History and Philosophical Society and the Ballymena Field Club. Towards the end of the last century the fields of Ulster were dug deep to extract the peat. The collectors include the Reverend I. Grainger of Broughshane, whose collection became the basis of the Ulster Museum. The Belfast engineer William Gray, and the Ballymena land agent William Knowles discovered a number of important sites. Flint-collecting was turned into a cottage industry. As early as 1891, William Wakeham wrote that the spirit of collection had increased, and that flints could command high prices. Counterfeit flints were eagerly purchased by Americans.

The tradition of collecting has provided indispensable archaeological evidence, which still survives today. It was a fieldworker that discovered the two most recent early Mesolithic sites in Ulster, near Dundonald, County Down.

The most famous early Mesolithic site in Ulster is Mount Sandel, near Coleraine, County Londonderry. People were living there about 7000 BC, and the site provides us with a great deal of knowledge about how man first came to Ireland. The site was first recognized in the 1880s by the collector William Gray. It was threatened with destruction by the expanding housing industry of the 1970s. The site was excavated by Peter Woodman, who took care that nothing of importance was lost. He had discovered at Mount Sandel the earliest man-made structures in Ireland. In a small hollow, huts had been erected – a Mesolithic community. Evidence for the erection of huts is provided by the pattern of post- and stake-holes, though with time the holes have been filled up with earth or, where a hut had burned down, by ash. The material filling the holes tends to be darker than the surrounding soil. At Mount Sandel the huts measured about 6 metres across, and each of them had a hearth in the centre. The post-holes were around the periphery of the huts. The hut was perhaps held together by poles or saplings dug into the earth. There is no trace of what material covered the walls, but they may have been covered with branches and skins, and there may have been an outer covering of earth to help keep out the cold. Several huts were erected in the same place, one after another, and this makes it difficult to establish the exact form of the huts, but it does indicate that the inhabitants of Mount Sandel returned to the site over a number of seasons. It is likely that this Mesolithic community moved from place to place throughout the year and came back to the same settlements. It is difficult to ascertain how many people lived in each hut. The activities of present-day hunter-gatherers suggest that six to nine people occupied each of the Mount Sandel huts.

Other huts were also discovered near Mount Sandel, but it is hard to determine if they were occupied at the same time as the huts described above. Peter Woodman discovered many pits in the ground that had probably been used to store food supplies. After they had served their purpose they acted as rubbish bins. These pits provide us with some indication of what the people of Mount Sandel ate. There were bones of mammals as well as fish, such as eels, salmon and trout, all of which were caught in the River Bann. Bird bones were also found, which points to the hunting or trapping of birds. Some pots held the charred remains of hazelnuts, which had probably been stored in them. Seeds of water lilies and wild apples were also discovered.

These discoveries help us to understand the conditions in this area at that time. People who live by hunting, fishing and gathering seldom live in the same place all year round. It is hard to find sufficient food in the same place throughout the four seasons, so they move around. Excavations at Mount Sandel have helped us to determine how the people there lived during the seasons.

Hazelnuts ripened in the autumn, so we deduce from their remains that people occupied Mount Sandel during that season. It is also possible that the site was occupied during the winter months, and the hazelnuts had been stored since the autumn.

Study of pig bones found at Mount Sandel shows that most of the pigs were juveniles when they were killed, and they were generally slaughtered during the late winter.

Study of the remains of salmon suggests that the community was fishing in spring and summer, while the bones of eels indicate autumn occupation, when the eels swim downstream. Peter Woodman suspected that the site was sometimes occupied for several seasons in succession. The site is probably situated to take advantage of available resources.

Peter Woodman excavated another early Mesolithic site at Castleroe, only 2 km from Mount Sandel. This was part of a community that settled around the estuary of the River Bann.

There is not much more to say about these early men, for there is very little evidence about their customs or social structure. For example, no burial site from the first 3,000 years of human settlement of Ireland has been discovered. However, it is safe to say that Mesolithic Ulster was a far cry from the system of earls, barons and Gaelic kings that flourished at a later date.

Societies of hunter-gatherers are egalitarian, and this means that autocracy is likely to have been the rule, and societies would have consisted of a number of families related to one another. Perhaps status was based upon age, sex, accomplishment or wisdom, but status would not necessarily equate to power. Leadership was by example rather than moral authority or physical coercion.

No other site in Ulster has yielded such an abundance of artefacts as Mount Sandel. The largest stone tools were flint axes, which were probably used for fashioning wooden tools. The axes appear in two forms: core axes and flake axes. The core axes have rounded, symmetrical edges that were sharpened by striking a blow across the edge. When the edge became dull from use, it was only necessary to knock another flint on the edge to sharpen it. These axes were used for chipping. The flake axe has a broad, straight edge and was made from a large flake. It was used for planing or chiselling. A number of adzes were also discovered.

The most common tool in the early Mesolithic period was the microlith.

Microliths are small splinters of flint, shaped for use. Those most frequently found are rods and needle points. They were manufactured by a technique called indirect percussion.

Flints of about 4 cm in length might be inserted into the end of a pointed wooden staff to make arrows or harpoons. They were also set into wooden handles to make saw-like instruments. Their small size makes these flints hard to find. They are sometimes discovered only when the soil is passed through a sieve. Excavation at Mount Sandel has uncovered over 1,000 shaped microliths, and over 6,000 small blades that might be fashioned into microliths.

Why are microliths of different shapes? Why were some implements made to look like rods or needle points? The triangular microliths were often found in pits that also contained pig bones, and this suggests that they might have been used as some form of weapon to hunt pigs. Once embedded in the pig, triangular microliths were hard to remove.

Large flints were also used to clean hides, since the edge could be used to scrape and work the skins of animals without damaging the surface of the hides. Scrapers were also found in other prehistoric sites. Fewer scrapers have been found at Mount Sandel than at comparable mainland sites, and this may be due to the small number of red deer in Ulster.

Burins have also been discovered. They were used to work bone and antlers into shape. Like the scrapers, they are few in number, and we can again conjecture that red deer were not a major prey of the Mount Sandel hunters.

Is Mount Sandel typical of early Mesolithic sites? Early Mesolithic sites typically occur in lowland areas, near rivers and lakes or on the sea coast. Survival was based on fishing, shellfish collecting, and trapping wild birds and mammals, particularly the wild pig. No Mesolithic sites have been discovered in the upland regions of Ulster, such as the Antrim Hills, the Mourne Mountains and the mountainous regions west of the River Bann, although the discovery of scrapers shows that prehistoric man may have occupied these areas in earlier times. Herds of red deer, the largest mammal that man could have hunted in the island, may have been commonest in these upland areas. The red deer was the main source of food for Mesolithic man in mainland Britain, but the number of red deer in Ireland may not have been sufficient to make them an important prey of the early colonists of Ireland. Red deer may have arrived in Ulster after colonization by man.

In springtime early Mesolithic families, or perhaps a single family, would camp near the sea, where there were supplies of fish and shellfish. Seabirds would be trapped. The coasts of counties Antrim and Down provided an important source of flint for making tools. In the summer and early autumn, families moved inland along the rivers and established camps in the best fishing places, such as where a river discharges into a lake. Plants were also gathered, and fish, such as salmon moving upstream, would be caught. Hazelnuts may have been important, for they could be easily stored to provide food in hard times. By the start of the winter, camps would have been fortified against harsh weather – Mount Sandel is perhaps a good example of the type of camp that Mesolithic people lived in during the winter. Late autumn was a good time to catch eels, and wild pigs became one of the main sources of food as the winter progressed. In spring the families would head back to the coast. This fits in with the evidence obtained from Mount Sandel, but it is important not to generalize from a single site. Examination of the bones of seal pups at Mount Sandel seems to suggest that they were killed in the winter; but at an early Mesolithic site in County Offaly they seem to have been killed in summer, when the animal would have been least mobile. Life involved seasonal movements of families, or small bands of several families together – it was quite an endurance test. Today societies of hunter-gatherers have prevailed in some of the harshest areas.

The Mesolithic communities were not only concerned with seeking out the next meal; they possessed their own rituals, beliefs, ceremonies and art.

It is not known for certain where the earliest colonists in Ulster originated. It has been thought that early man may have come from the west of Scotland, across the sea to counties Antrim and Down. There are numerous sites in Antrim and Down which seem to indicate that the early inhabitants of Ulster came from Scotland. There is no evidence that man occupied Scotland any earlier than Ireland. It has been proposed that hunter-gathering communities may have walked from France to the southern coast of Britain and crossed into Ireland. But is this explanation likely? There are similarities between the Stone Age dwellers in Ireland and those in Britain. Evidence in Britain occurs later than in Ulster, but it is possible that new discoveries will push back the date of the earliest warrior-like activity in the north of Ireland. At the time of the colonization of Ireland, the level of the Irish Sea would have been quite low, and it is thought that the land was exposed all the way to the Isle of Man. From the Isle of Man it is possible to see the

Mourne Mountains. Ireland was ripe for conquest. The people who crossed the Irish Sea to occupy Ulster were coastal dwellers, experienced in making and using boats. Perhaps relics of some of these early colonists lie at the bottom of the Irish Sea or are still preserved on the Isle of Man.

Some of the first settlers in Ulster would have crossed the North Channel and the Irish Sea in dugout canoes or skin-covered vessels. They might not have crossed to Ireland in great numbers. A single boat of about twenty-five people would have been insufficient to have sustained a viable population that would have survived to colonize all of Ireland. It is likely that a number of people tried to settle in the north over a number of years. It is likely that they landed on the South Down or Leinster coasts. They eventually spread out from those centres across all of Ireland, wherever coastal and river resources permitted settlement. They reached the Blackwater region of Munster and as far inland as County Offaly, but most of the evidence of these first colonists of Ireland is found in the north of Ulster.

During the Mesolithic period, tools were refined and developed. In the early Mesolithic some tools were abandoned and men started to fashion large implements from long, hard stones. A piece of stone might be found on a beach and used as a striking platform. A stone tool could be fashioned in a few seconds by striking a hard stone, such as quartzite, against the platform. As well as large stone flakes, the earlier axes, which were flaked from stone, started to disappear. They were eventually replaced by axes made from schist and baked mudstone, whose surfaces had been polished. It is difficult to account for these changes since many of them appear to indicate a shift from sophisticated stone implements in the earlier period to much simpler tools. It has been suggested that the early Mesolithic people died out or were replaced by a seasonal wave of colonists, who brought their simple tools with them. However, this is very unlikely since the later Mesolithic tools are almost exclusively found in Ireland and the Isle of Man; they are unlikely to be found in Britain or on the Continent. It is not known where the new tools came from. Perhaps the later Mesolithic people of Ireland were descended from their predecessors.

In Ulster, communities came to settle and work nodules of flint along the coast from 5500 BC onwards. However, the late Mesolithic is characterized by heavy battering waves and a rise in sea level. Then the land itself started to rise and there was a corresponding fall in the sea level. Conditions became stable again and the beaches of the later Mesolithic in Ulster were about 8 metres above present-day levels. These coastal sites were studied as long ago as 1865 by collectors, such as William Gray of Belfast. Other sites in County Antrim, especially those around the Larne, were visited by the Belfast Naturalists' Field Club. Fierce debate broke out as to whether these were remains of Palaeolithic man in Ulster. William Knowles, the Ballymena estate agent, proved to be one of Ulster's greatest collectors. He declared that the stone or flint implements found buried on the beaches were most likely to be evidence of the last people still to be using stone tools in the British Isles. Others, like Gray himself, believed that they dated to the New Stone Age. It was shown that the flint flakes were deposited after the end of the last ice age and therefore they could not be Palaeolithic.

A great deal of material was found at Larne – called the Larnian Culture and excavated by Hallam Movius of Harvard University. In 1933, at Curran Point at Larne, he recovered 15,000 flints from the raised beach. Heavily battered and rolled flakes were scattered along the coasts that were already producing flints with large, hard hammer stones. Excavations at Bay Farm, near Carnlough, County Antrim, revealed later Mesolithic flint in good condition.

The coastal sites provide us with the best evidence for later Mesolithic communities in the north of Ireland, though they mainly appear to have been occupied for only a few days each year. The sites provide us with information about these early peoples, for here are battered remains of the flint-working stations. Most of the sites are situated near rivers. The most important of these is at Newferry, County Antrim. Peter Woodman excavated some sites situated where Lough Beg empties into the River Bann. Here there were good conditions for Mesolithic fishermen. Later Mesolithic communities occupied these sites, now and again, for nearly 2,000 years, from about 5500 BC to 3500 BC. The tools that accumulated in the earth are typical of this region, and the development of late

Mesolithic tools can be traced in various layers of the sites.

The later Mesolithic hunters and fishermen utilized as their main tool flints from the River Bann, and many thousands have been found along the river. One such tool is a simple leaf-shaped flake that looks like a spearhead whose butt has been trimmed. The technical name for such a tool is a butt-trimmed flake. These tools are quite common in County Antrim, and they are by no means limited to the Bann Valley. They have been discovered throughout Ireland, but they are mostly found along the riverbanks or near the sea coast. The butt is often too thick to have been easily attached to anything as slender as an arrow shaft or spear shaft. Some authorities believe that they were mounted on a wooden handle and that they served as all-purpose hunting-and-fishing knives. These tools were used in many different ways. Close examination of these implements may provide us with some evidence about the lives of these peoples.

As well as flint tools, there were also axes made out off schist or mudstone. Such axes were made by using flint to flake the axe into shape and by grinding down the surface by rubbing it against an abrasive stone, such as sandstone. Mudstone axes are very interesting, for this stone is mainly found along a belt of territory from County Down to County Longford in the south of Ireland.

Flint tools of course have been found along the banks of the River Bann, and the flints used in making them came from coastal sites in County Antrim, up to 30 km away. Unlike the coastal sites, the inland sites, such as Newferry, reveal, almost exclusively, finished tools. The coastal sites provided not only sea implements, but also flint tools such as those found at the inland river sites. Unworked flint was not carried from the inland or coastal sites over any great distance. This pattern can be observed in North-East Ulster, but the same cannot be said of Southern Ulster, where the axes originated. Here there is not much evidence of Mesolithic sites of any sort. The people who occupied the riverbanks of Northern Ulster also made seasonal visits to counties Fermanagh and Tyrone to collect stone for making the axes. Perhaps the western regions of Ulster were better settled than contemporary evidence suggests. They may have exchanged their stone axes for supplies of flint.

Fishing seems to have been the basis of the Mesolithic way of life, and the rivers of Donegal may have attracted abundant Mesolithic settlement. Amateur archaeologists in Fermanagh, Donegal, Monaghan and Cavan have undertaken surveys in areas where they might expect to find evidence of Mesolithic communities, but flakes and worked mudstone have proved hard to find. There are no scrapers for cleaning hide or burins for working bone and antler. At Mesolithic sites across the Irish Sea in Britain, an abundance of scrapers has been found – most likely used for cleaning the hides of red deer and wild cattle. Red deer seem to have been of minor importance to the late Mesolithic communities of Ulster; wild cattle were absent from Ireland. It is likely that a huge range of bone and wooden implements has not survived.

In 1937 Adolf Mahr, the keeper of Irish Antiquities in the National Museum of Ireland in Dublin, published a thorough analysis of Riverford cattle. Quantities of schist and mudstone axes were uncovered. They were each carved from a single block of stone. Clubs have mainly been recovered from along major riverbanks, especially those of the River Bann at Culbane and Portglenone, and also along the coasts. A club of greywacke, measuring 40 cm long, was found by chance on the shores of St John's Point, County Down. The purpose of the club is not clear. Similar clubs have been found in other European fishing communities. They may have been used to stun or kill very large fish.

Most Mesolithic sites are situated along the coasts and on the flood plains of rivers such as the Bann. The fish were perhaps the most important food. Maybe flint, bone and wood were used for making fish-spears and harpoons. Several hundred axes were found at Culbane, which suggests a great attempt at woodworking along the River Bann. At Toome Bay, County Londonderry, where the River Bann joins Lough Neagh, later Mesolithic material was recovered from the peat in 1930 by Claude Blake Whelan, a lawyer. He became one of the foremost amateur authorities on ancient settlements in Ulster. In 1950 Trinity College Dublin made its contribution: Frank Mitchell undertook to excavate the site, and the remains of several implements of hazel and pine were uncovered, some of which may have been shafts for fishing or hunting weapons.

No matter how hard were the times, it does not seem that the later Mesolithic people had degenerated; rather, they had undergone change. The Mesolithic people in Ireland seem to have been entirely dependent on stone tools, whereas, after the start of the Mesolithic, there is only a little evidence for subsequent excavation of flints in Britain. This might reflect a stagnant society, except that sites in Ulster indicate a vibrant community that survived for nearly 2,000 years.

Why was there such a dramatic change in technology between the early and late Mesolithic periods? Several answers have been put forward, but not all are convincing. Man may have started to hunt the red deer, and this may have required a change of weapon. This appears to be unlikely, for the weapons used in the early Mesolithic to kill wild boar could handle deer as well. The scarcity of scrapers in the late Mesolithic also indicates that the red deer were still not of much importance.

The change of tools might also be due to an increase in sources of flint. In the Antrim region there was an abundance of flint, so the earlier, more economical, tool-making methods became redundant. However, we find the less-sophisticated, more wasteful method used everywhere in the late Mesolithic – even in areas that did not have abundant sources of flint.

There may have been some cultural reasons why the population of Ireland changed its way of life. Ireland's isolation from the British mainland and Continental Europe during the later Mesolithic meant that it was free to develop its own industries, but this is a very dubious conclusion. The real explanation may remain unknown. The Mesolithic sites – those between 6,000 BC (when we see the microliths) and about 5500 BC – show the appearance of later Mesolithic tools.

We must return to the site at Newferry where weather conditions had taken their toll. Here, clay pots and leaf-shaped arrowheads have been discovered – evidence that new colonists had arrived in Ulster to change the shape of the landscape.

Chapter 2

The First Farmers

The second wave of colonists reached Ulster about 4000 BC. Thousands of years earlier, in South-East Asia, people had abandoned a life based mainly on hunting and gathering. They had gradually developed a way of life centred on agriculture and the rearing of domestic animals. A settled way of life favoured the growth of villages, and an increase in the population. This may have prompted farmers to move into South-East Europe. Over many generations these farmers made their way slowly across Europe, influencing the local population of hunter-gatherers to adopt the new system. By about 4500 BC farmers were known along the Atlantic coast, and soon afterwards they reached Britain and Ireland.

These colonists brought with them something new. They had greater control over their food resources and seasonal movements were no longer necessary. They lived in permanent settlements all year round. These farmers introduced a number of domestic animals into Ireland – cattle, sheep, goats and pigs. With the exception of pigs, all these species were new to the island – at least since the end of the last ice age. They must have impressed the indigenous population in Ulster! Domestic cattle must have come with a shock! The earlier plant diet, which included hazelnuts and water-lily seeds, was greatly increased by the addition of cereals, such as wheat and barley.

The first farmers also brought new technology. They introduced their own variety of polished-stone axes (used for clearing forests), grinding stones (for processing cereals) and pots made from clay (for cooking and to be used as containers). The type of tools used in hunting also changed as the newcomers brought their own weapons – flint arrowheads and javelins. Now there was easy access to animals whose hides were useful to man, and, as a result, there is an abundance of flint scrapers from this time onwards. The inhabitants of Ulster now began to bury their dead and hold religious services in and about the stone monuments that still dot the landscape.

These changes are a radical departure from the way of life of the earliest Mesolithic. Archaeologists name this period the Neolithic or New Stone Age. There has been much debate amongst archaeologists about this period – whether the introduction of the Neolithic way of life in Ulster was brought about by new colonists, or whether the local community simply picked up new ideas that were spreading throughout Europe and Britain at this time – but the evidence points to movements from Britain by sea.

A way of life based on cattle, sheep and goats became the norm, as the new ideas infiltrated. These animals had to be shipped across the sea into Ulster and the rest of Ireland. The same is true of cereal crops, which first appear in Ireland during the Neolithic.

Some still suggest that the new economy was introduced by local Mesolithic populations rather than the farmer-colonists. According to this theory the local Mesolithic population in Ulster may well have come into contact with farming peoples on the other side of the Irish Sea. They may also have learnt about the new cereals from them.

However, the later Mesolithic people appear to be culturally isolated from developments in Britain. It is most unlikely that seasonal hunter-gatherers were able immediately to adopt the complicated and radically new techniques of a settled agriculture-based lifestyle. The fact that agricultural communities appeared in Ulster at the same time as Britain suggests that a new people spread rapidly through the whole of the British Isles. It is likely that with their new way of life they also introduced a new language and a new religion.

One of the earliest farms in the British Isles can be found at Ballynagilly, County Tyrone. Here a Neolithic farmer established a farm on a small hill, and the site was excavated by Arthur Simon. He discovered the remains of a house measuring 6.5 by 6 metres. It was an all-year-round settlement, and the building was constructed along the lines of those at Mount Sandel. The longer sides of the dwelling were lined with trenches into which upright oak planks were placed to serve as walls. There were post-holes not only around the edges of the house but also within the dwelling. The roof was made out of pitch and the interior posts held up the centre of the roof. Within the house there were traces of a hearth and maybe an oven. The house had been burned and ash from the walls yielded a radiocarbon date of about 3700 BC. Many pits were also discovered, and hearths that date from the Neolithic period.

Ballynagilly is a single site, but it is not certain if it is typical of sites in the early Neolithic. It is not known if there were farms similar to Ballynagilly outside Ulster.

Another house, discovered at Ballyglass in County Mayo, measured 13 by 6 metres; and the largest of several Neolithic houses excavated near Tankardstown in County Limerick measured 13 by 7 metres. A short distance away stood another house, 7 by 4.4 metres. A number of other sites have been excavated in Ireland. This evidence points to a pattern of settlement called dispersed settlement. The clustering of farms into villages, common in Europe but perhaps unknown in Ireland at this time, is known as nucleated settlement. The general rule was that people in Ireland lived in dispersed settlements.

It is possible that sites were not as stable or did not exist for as long as the one at Ballynagilly. In the sand dunes of Dundrum, County Down, Pat Collins discovered Neolithic pottery and flint tools which suggest that there was a Neolithic settlement nearby. We have no idea how permanent this settlement was. Neolithic pottery has also been found at White Park Bay. County Antrim. Other objects have been found at the Madman's Window, near Glenarm, County Antrim. Settlements were often situated near a source of flint for tools.

Recently Derek Simpson has excavated a Neolithic site at

Ballygally, County Antrim. Inland lakes served as areas of Neolithic settlement. Fragments of Neolithic pottery were uncovered by Oliver Davies at Island MacHugh, County Tyrone. There are traces of small Neolithic settlements in County Tyrone and Lough Enagh, County Londonderry. At Carnlough, County Antrim, there are traces of farmsteads both along the coast at Bay Farm and also in the windy region of Windy Ridge, near Lough-na-Trosk. Upland sites, such as this, may have been associated with the seasonal movement of livestock into higher pastures – a common practice throughout Ireland's history. These examples seem to indicate a change in the settlement patterns of Ulster, for almost all the former settlements were confined to the sea coast and river valleys. Neolithic Ulstermen were able to settle in regions that had escaped the attention of the Mesolithic.

Not all evidence points to small settlement sites in Ulster. Two of the largest enclosed Neolithic settlements in Ireland were situated in County Antrim, near Templepatrick, on either side of the Six Mile Water. The largest is at Lyles Hill, which was excavated by Estyn Evans of Queen's University. The site, measuring about 385 by 210 metres, is situated on a large hill. The entire hilltop was surrounded by an earthen bank, which Evans thought dated from the Neolithic. More recently, Derek Simpson of Queen's University re-excavated the site and concluded that the earthworks probably dated from the Bronze Age or Iron Age and not earlier. He discovered fortifications that Evans had missed. The top of the hill was defended by two lines of palisades – an inner palisaded bank, from about 3000 BC, and an outer defence, erected between 3800 BC and 2400 BC.

During the excavation of Lyles Hill, Estyn Evans discovered pits, hearths, a lot of Neolithic pottery, stone tools and stone ornaments. Much of the material was recovered from an area of ash which had been covered by a stone cairn. Hoards of pottery, flint and bones may have been deposited there as part of some sort of ceremony. Excavations elsewhere on the hilltop, and outside the area of the cairn, have uncovered much pottery and flint; all of these seem to suggest that there was an important settlement at Lyles Hill.

Some miles north of Lyles Hill stretches the larger Donegore Hill, at the summit of which are the remains of a defensive enclosure. Neolithic sites have been partly excavated here. The hilltop was surrounded not only by palisades but also by two ditches. However, they may not all date from the same period. This site is smaller that the one at Lyles Hill. It measures 200 by 150 metres.

Barrie Hartwell of Queen's University discovered the ditches at Donegore Hill when he photographed the hill from the air. Aerial photography is widely used throughout Ireland, and Lyles Hill was one of the first sites discovered by this method. Donegore Hill, however, has a better example of a protective ditch, even though it could only be seen from the air. Before it was excavated it was found that the soil in the ditch was better able to retain water than the surrounding soil, so during a dry summer the surrounding crop would turn yellow-brown, while the crop growing where the ditch once was remained greener. The colour difference was not noticeable from the ground. Now it has been excavated to a depth of 1 to 2 metres and 3 metres across.

A striking feature of the Donegore Hill is that it is of solid basalt and yet the ditch was originally excavated without the use of metal tools. The excavation of such ditches is common in the chalk hills of Southern Britain, where circular-ditch enclosures are properly known as causewayed camps. The ditches were dug with antler picks. No antler picks have survived at Donegore, but it is likely that a similar technique was used here. With an antler pick, Neolithic man could have removed a large basketful of basalt in about ten minutes.

More implements were discovered within the site than at Lyles Hill, and radiocarbon dating of what seemed to be the remains of horses suggests that this site was occupied in the Neolithic from about 4000 BC to 2700 BC. The site at Donegore may be older that the one at Lyles Hill, but by about 3000 BC both sites were occupied.

There is some evidence that Neolithic people did engage in warfare. At Crickley Hill in England there is evidence of an assault on the enclosure. At the Six Mile Water site evidence is not so clear, but less than 5% of the site has been excavated. At Donegore the ditches seem to have posed a psychological barrier rather than a physical one. Ditches have been used everywhere in the world to mark the extremities of settlements. It has been suggested that the ditch may have been put under divine protection, so a would-be attacker would not dare to leap across it. Graffiti in present-day Northern Ireland sometimes affords a similar kind of psychological barrier to would-be intruders. In early Roman history Romulus is said to have executed Remus as a punishment for jumping across the walls that bounded early Rome.

Some traces of Neolithic buildings have survived to the present day. Pits have been discovered on numerous sites, as well as the occasional hearth. Evidence of Neolithic settlement is far more widespread in Ireland than on the Continent. At Goodland, County Antrim, a Neolithic settlement consisted of a small ditch and more than 120 pits of various sizes. Both the ditch and the pits have been filled with cobbles, ash, sherds of pottery and flints. It has been suggested that in Neolithic Ireland, perhaps during fertility ceremonies, debris was taken from around habitations and thrown into pits. Some archaeologists have accepted this idea, whilst others argue that the pits in Neolithic sites were filled with rubbish. There is no proof that they originated in a religious ceremony. Ditches are found at other Neolithic sites, such as one on the borders of Lough Neagh, where Dudley Waterman of the Archaeological Survey of Northern Ireland discovered traces of a Neolithic settlement. Chris Lynn, who excavated on Scotch Street in the heart of Armagh, found an enclosure measuring about 12 metres across and 1 metre deep. Neolithic pottery dating from around 2800 BC was also found here. It is not known what the ditch was used for. Chris Lynn suggested that some of the 'ritual' explanations might suffice until a better understanding is reached.

Another Neolithic settlement in Armagh has brought forth new information. Here Dudley Waterman uncovered traces of a Neolithic settlement, including about twenty pits and many flints. However, the Neolithic settlement covered only a small area. This site eventually became Emain Macha, the ancient capital of Ulster.

Despite the large number of sites, we still know very little about Neolithic communities in Ireland. Most remains have long ago been destroyed. There are some remains at Mount Sandel, where carbonization of wheat and barley has rendered them resistant to further decay.

At another Neolithic site, Dooey's Cairn, a megalithic tomb in County Antrim, the impressions of thirteen spikelets of wheat have been found.

What about domestic animals? Scattered remains of sheep, goats and pigs as well as dogs have been found in a few sites. Dairy farming was not known in Ulster until the Iron Age.

The Neolithic farmers were the first inhabitants of Ulster to make an impact upon the land. In order to grow crops and provide pasturage, it was necessary to clear the virgin forests. In some cases the land reverted to forest or passed into bogland. One scientific technique that helps us to understand man's first impact upon Ulster is pollen analysis, or palynology.

Sufferers from hay fever will know about the pollen count. The amount of pollen in the air fluctuates according to the season, weather conditions and the types of plants in a given area. Examination of ancient pollen grains in materials like peat can give us an idea of the conditions that prevailed thousands of years ago and the species of plants that flourished then.

At the Neolithic sites of Ballynagilly and Beaghmore in County Tyrone, Fallyhogy in County Londonderry and Ballyscullian in County Antrim, a study of pollen grains tells us that sometime around 3800 BC there was a drop in the amount of pollen from trees such as oak, pine, hazel and, especially, elm. At the same time there was a rise in grass pollen. Not infrequently particles of ash found with the pollen can be dated to this period. Neolithic farmers had moved into virgin forest, cutting down and burning trees, and cereal crops had been planted on the cleared land. In folklore the clearing of the forests was attributed to Partholan, around 2600 BC.

To find out how forested Ireland was during the Neolithic, we can look at the percentage of tree pollen in the atmosphere. In present-day Ulster, tree pollen makes up only 15% of the total, whereas in the Neolithic tree pollen amounted to 80 to 90% of the total. By about 1,000 years ago it had fallen to 30%. Ulster forests have been steadily declining for the past 5,000 years, and their most dramatic reduction was during the prehistoric period. The modern Ulster landscape owes its condition to its prehistoric inhabitants.

Pollen records also show the pattern of settlement. Jonathan Pilcher, working for Queen's University Belfast, has undertaken a comparative study of the sites that reveal clear evidence of "landram". Many sites show a similar pattern: cereal cultivation followed by several centuries of open landscape but without evidence for cereals. Pilcher has suggested that this shows a shift from arable to pastoral farming. Towards the later Neolithic the forests regenerated. The inhabitants abandoned their earlier areas of settlement and moved on.

Where a Neolithic tomb is found, it is probable that there were settlements in the same area; it is thus possible to identify the areas of Ulster where the Neolithic population was densest. Gabriel Cooney has carried out a similar survey in County Leitrim. In general, megalithic tombs can be found on well-drained soil between 120 and 240 metres above sea level. Good soil was important. Many of these tombs are now situated in areas covered by heath or bog, but during the Neolithic these regions were drained and easy to work. Sally Kish discovered that cereal pollen at an altitude of 485 metres on Slieve Croob, County Down, dated to between 3600 BC and 3200 BC. This pattern of settlement, with arable farming in upland regions began to change during the Bronze Age.

Neolithic fields walls, built from stone, are also of great interest. How is it possible to date a prehistoric wall? These early walls are often covered with peat, and it is possible to use radiocarbon dating to find out the age of the peat lying immediately above the base of the wall. The most extensive field system in the island was in County Mayo. Here, for the past twenty years, Seamus Caulfield of University College Dublin has investigated field walls which date to the Neolithic period. The Mayo field system covers over 250 square km along the North Mayo coast. Field boundaries of stone (and also earthen walls) have been uncovered. Ceide Fields is a 100-hectare monument, extending over several townlands. The walls were used to divide the landscape into long fields, not to enclose one field after another in a crazy fashion. The long walls in the valley bottom follow the contours closely, but walls higher up the slopes ignore the terrain in order to be parallel with those lower down. The fields were probably used to enclose cattle. Fifty to sixty families may have lived in the area – something in the order of 300 people – but there is no evidence of a village. This planned network of fields, which suggests a well-organized society, seems in contrast to the idea of individual farmsteads separated from one another by thick forests.

It is not likely that much of the early Ulster landscape was divided into strips of land in this way. However, where parts of the Neolithic landscape have been well-preserved under bog for the past 4,000 years, these is a little evidence that field walls were built in Ulster in the Neolithic. A field wall, possibly dating to the later Neolithic, was discovered on the Galboly plateau, near Carnlough, on the Antrim coast. There is also a little evidence that flint works can be dated to a later period elsewhere in Ulster. Fieldwork is still in its infancy, but there is reason to be optimistic. For some years investigations within Central Ulster, notably in County Tyrone, have pointed to a Neolithic presence, and excavations have revealed field boundaries disappearing beneath bogs. As in North Mayo, there may be a Neolithic landscape buried under the blanket of the Ulster uplands.

Chapter 3

Neolithic Times

Prehistoric flint flakes and waste material as well as broken pieces of ancient pottery are not uncommon in many parts of Ulster, and this invites anyone in the province to follow prehistoric archaeology.

The Neolithic settlers cleared the forests using axes of polished stone or flint. In Ulster the axes were sometimes also made from a volcanic stone known as porcellanite. It occurs in two regions in Ulster: Brockley, on Rathlin Island in County Antrim, and the more well-known site of Tievebulliagh, near Cushendall, also in County Antrim. The manufacture of these axes involved several different processes, and the first of these is extraction. At Tievebulliagh, outcrops of slightly black porcellanite occur on the face of the mountain. Broken pieces of porcellanite probably lay about the area, but the Neolithic men probably also used brute force to cause pieces to fracture and break off. Larger pieces of porcellanite were broken into workable sizes and fashioned into axes, probably using quartzite (which can still be found around Tievebulliagh) as hammer stones. William Knowles, the Ballymena estate agent who discovered the Tievebulliagh axe factory, is said to have carried off cartloads of axes. Half-finished axes are known as 'roughouts', and roughouts have been found in the area of the mountain. There was a considerable industry at Tievebulliagh.

The roughouts were rubbed against an abrasive stone, such as sandstone, until they were smooth and polished. At Culbane in County Londonderry porcellanite axes and a sandstone grinding block were found. It could take hours or even days to make a polished axe. Neolithic axe-makers polished the entire surface of the axe and not only the working edge. These tools were used with or without wooden handles, but of course the wooden handles have not survived in any great quantity. Neolithic polished stone axes, complete with their wooden handles, have been recovered from waterlogged sites on the Continent, and in Ulster complete axes and handles have been found at Maguire's Bridge, County Fermanagh, and in County Monaghan.

The only way for archaeologists to test the effectiveness of the axes was to use them to cut down trees. Three Danish archaeologists using polished stone axes were able to clear 500 metres of birch forest in five hours. A Russian archaeologist cut down pine trees measuring 25 cm in diameter in an average of about twenty minutes per tree. These axes, the primary tools of the earlier farmers in Ulster, were highly effective for tree-felling.

Porcellanite axes manufactured at Rathlin Island or Tievebulliagh were exported all over Ireland. Alison Sheridan of the National Museum of Scotland in Edinburgh has carried out a survey of these finds – about 1,400 axes altogether. One hundred and sixty porcellanite axes have been found in Scotland, Wales and England. Axes manufactured in Britain have been found in Ulster. In County Antrim, axes manufactured in the Great Langdale factory in Cumbria have been discovered at Cushendall, Portglenone and other places. An axe from the Graig Llwyd factory in North Wales was discovered at Lyles Hill.

It is unknown what the rate of exchange was for these axes. The highest density of axe finds is in County Antrim; it is almost saturated with porcellanite axes. Archaeologists talk of 'supply zones' and a simple form of trade known as 'down the line', whereby one community obtained a certain number of axes and passed them on to distant communities.

Some axes were never meant to be used. Axes in the Malone Hoard in the Ulster Museum are too long to have been used by Neolithic man. These axes measure 20 to 38 cm long and would have required someone like Finn MacCool to lift them. These large axes were probably more symbolic than practical. They might have been an indication of wealth, power or religion.

Forty stone mace heads have been recovered in Ireland – nearly half of these in Ulster. These maces were manufactured out of stone such as gneiss and amphibolite mounted on a wooden shaft. These too are likely to have been an indication of the owner's status. They were found in Northern and Eastern Ireland and were comparable with those in Northern Britain, especially the Orkney Islands. This points to considerable intercourse between Britain and Ireland in these early centuries.

The exchange of axes was not only a commercial affair. In recent times anthropologists have studied communities who use and exchange stone axes, and they have noted that axes have also been used as engagement gifts, included in dowries and so on. Axes may have been exchanged for favours as well as goods.

The sale of counterfeit polished stones and axes was a lucrative local industry in Ulster during the nineteenth century. In a letter to *The Ulster Journal of Archaeology*, published in 1857, a correspondent noted that one of the guides at the Giant's Causeway had been caught polishing up a basalt axe. The correspondent also claimed that there was a large industry in counterfeit prehistoric artefacts. Weavers often employed smooth stones for flattening materials, and when natural stones were not available the weavers would make their own. Such stones look very much like prehistoric tools and even experts were fooled.

Throughout the period, Neolithic sites, especially along the Antrim coast, continued to be exploited. Flint nodules were shaped, flakes would be struck off them, and they would be fashioned into tools. Open-cast quarries along the Antrim coast at Ballygally and in the Black Mountain near Belfast were also exploited.

Flints might have been exported, and we believe there was a coastal trade in flint by the late Mesolithic – for instance, at Dunaff Bay on the Inishowen Peninsula in County Donegal. Laurence Flanagan has commented several times on the discovery of rich flints elsewhere in Donegal, near Raphoe and in the court tombs at Bayan. As with the trade in stone axes, we occasionally find foreign substitutes in Ulster sites. Pitchstone from the Aran Islands in Western Scotland has been discovered at Lyles Hill and Ballygally for some unknown reason. Some of the Antrim flints were found in Scotland, near Portpatrick and Campbeltown. These include leaf-shaped arrowheads, which were perhaps the main weapon used in hunting and warfare. The arrowheads were made thin and sharp by the technique of pressure-flaking.

Flint javelin heads have been found in Ireland. These can be distinguished from arrowheads since they are much larger – about 5 cm in width and perhaps 25 cm in length. They are more robust than arrowheads. Pat Collins has made a study of the javelin heads; he concluded that they were probably designed to be attached to shafts for throwing rather than for thrusting like spears. The distribution of spears in Ireland is mainly confined to Ulster. They have been found on settlement sites and in tombs. They can also be found in Southern Britain. The flint knife was another common tool in Neolithic Ireland. It was normally flat on one side and curved on the other: it is known as the plano-convex knife. They have also been found in sentiments and tombs.

With the raising of cattle and, to a lesser degree, sheep, scrapers, like those found at Mesolithic sites, assumed a greater importance. Both scrapers and knives were used in the fashioning of hides. We can also see the development of a new form of scraper called a hollow scraper. Its function remains a mystery. Some archaeologists think that they may have been used as saws for cutting bone. In County Tyrone, 120 hollow scrapers were discovered; another thirty were uncovered at Lyles Hill. They have also been found in hoards. At Killybeg, County Antrim, a hoard of sixty-five scrapers and blades of various sizes was discovered.

Where flint tools are found together it can be conjectured that they were being transported as part of the flint trade, which had existed since Mesolithic times. Flint was being made into a variety of tools in Neolithic Ulster, but the methods were similar to those used in the manufacture of the polished stone axe.

The first farmers in Ulster had introduced pottery, and their pottery can provide us with information about how they lived and their relationship with other peoples. Pottery can also help us in the dating of sites. Now let's take a look at the manufacture of ceramic pots.

It is not certain, but it is probable, that the manufacture of pots in Neolithic Ulster was the work of women. Pottery was basically a domestic craft. Clay would be rolled into strands, which were then built up in coils to make the pots. The pots were smoothed on the outside, and a small stone or piece of bone might be rubbed against the outer surface of each pot to give it a polished appearance. The pots were then allowed to dry naturally before they were fired. This was carried out on bonfires and not in sophisticated kilns. Where the pots were fired without access to oxygen (for example, if they were completely buried in the ash), they would turn out dark-brown or black; where they were exposed to the air during firing, the surface would oxidize and turn orange.

Society had become more complex and there are almost certain to have been craft specialists, such as full-time potters, in Ulster at this time.

Flint artefacts have been collected since the nineteenth century, but our knowledge of Neolithic pottery began at a later date. In 1927, R. S. Macalister wrote that the only examples of Neolithic pottery were in the collection of the Royal Irish Academy – one bowl from Clones, County Monaghan, and another one from Donegore, County Antrim. However, an extensive collection of pottery from the Stone Age has since been discovered. Early pottery comes into two main categories: Western Neolithic and Lyles Hill ware. The first name derives from the fact that there was a broad similarity in Neolithic pottery all over the Atlantic fringe of Western Europe. The second category derives its name from Lyles Hill, where, with Donegore Hill, the largest hoard of Neolithic pottery has been found. The fact that potters first appeared at the beginning of the Neolithic provides us with yet another name – Neolithic 'A' ware.

Lyles Hill ware is of a simple kind, with few decorations. Occasionally small knobs for handling the pots have been found. Lyles Hill pottery has similarities with Grimston ware, which is typical of the early pottery of Northern England. This supports the theory that the earliest occupants of Ulster came from Northern Britain.

The later Neolithic sees the appearance of a different style of pottery (Neolithic 'B' ware), which is often decorated. Michael Herity of University College Dublin has carried out some excavations and identified three new types of pottery, some of which is quite elaborate.

The first are necked vessels, called Ballyalton bowls after pottery found in a tomb at Ballyalton, County Down. These bowls have a small neck and a very wide shoulder. The surfaces are decorated with incisions or cord impressions. These necked vessels have been found at roughly thirty sites, about half of which are in Ulster.

The second type comprises a series of broad-rimmed vessels, decorated with small channels and impressions or small dots. These pots have been recovered in coastal sand dunes near Newcastle, County Down. This type of pottery has sometimes been called Sandhills ware. The pottery is more circular than Lyles Hill ware, and seems to have been made by the local Mesolithic population who still occupied the coasts after the arrival of the farmers. Approximately twenty-five sites have yielded Sandhills ware, and nearly 70% of these lie in Ulster.

The third type of pottery consists of small globular bowls, decorated with cord incisions and impressions. A comprehensive hoard of these pots was found at Goodland, County Antrim, and they are known as Goodland bowls. About thirty-six sites have yielded Goodland bowls, and all but two of them are in Ulster.

There is also a type of pottery called Carrowkeel ware, which takes its name from a passage-tomb cemetery at Carrowkeel, County Sligo. Carrowkeel ware has a globular shape and is decorated with grooves.

The different styles perhaps reflect change with the passage of time. The early vessels at Lyles Hill were plain and undecorated, and these give way to decorated pots, which may sometimes indicate the status of the owner, and which are generally found in burial tombs. Declaration gradually became the norm as time progressed. It is hard to say if the nature of the pots was the same in the rest of Ireland. Some sites have yielded a single type of pot; others, such as Ballykeel, County Armagh, have yielded examples of nearly every form of Neolithic pot. We are still a long way from a complete understanding of Neolithic pottery.

There are few textile remains in Ulster originating from the Neolithic; Greenstone beads and pendants have been recovered from megalithic tombs and settlements, such as Lyles Hill and Donegore Hill. Some other beads from Lyles Hill have been identified as serpentine. They were probably imported from the Continent. Long antler pins to fasten cloaks and shawls have been uncovered in passage tombs.

Woolly sheep did not appear until the close of the Neolithic in Eastern Europe, and they would not have arrived in Ulster until after the end of the Neolithic, so weaving did not develop until then. Funeral rituals too do not seem to have become important until after the prehistoric period.

Tombs were constructed from large stones called megaliths (Greek *mega* 'large' *lithos* 'stone'). They were common in Northern Europe and all along the Atlantic coast, from Spain and Portugal in the south to Denmark and Southern Sweden in the north. In the British Isles they are found mainly in the north and west, where they can be seen in Wales, Scotland and Ireland. Why these stones were used for tombs is not known. The tombs may have marked the boundaries of territory. During the Mesolithic, hunter-gatherers would have had no conception of personal ownership of land. Agricultural societies, however, depend upon ownership of certain good portions of land, and communities have to mark their territories.

Archaeologists examining tombs in Ireland have come across monuments which seem to date from different periods. It is difficult to say if they represent different societies or even different peoples. The precise date of these tombs is not known. There are four major types that will be examined.

The first are court tombs. Archaeologists include Irish megalithic tombs in this category. They generally include three basic elements:

1. A stone gallery for burials, divided into from two to five chambers, often separated from one another by a single flat stone.

2. A forecourt at the entrance of the gallery, formed of a series of stones in an arc. It is the forecourt that gives the tombs their present names – court tombs or court cairns – though sometimes they are also called horned cairns. The stones that form the court are usually set upright and are known as orthostats (Greek *orthos* 'straight' *statos* 'standing'). Sometimes only a few standing stones were set up at intervals, and the spaces between them were filled with stone using the 'post and panel' method.

3. An earthwork or stone cairn, which usually had a trapezoidal shape, enclosing the area behind the forecourt, including the gallery.

These tombs were usually directed with the entrance facing east.

There are over 390 court tombs in Ireland, and these occur mostly in the north of the island, in a line drawn from Carlingford to Sligo. Similar tombs are found in Western Scotland, but some archaeologists have put these into a different category. We rely mainly upon the work of Estyn Evans and Oliver Davies, who studied Neolithic Ulster tombs in the 1930s and 1940s. They had a budget of about £10 so they had very little money to pay their assistants. The form of the tombs varies considerably throughout Ulster. The tombs they investigated include those at Clady Halliday, County Tyrone; Cohaw, County Cavan; Audleystown, County Down; and Farran Macbride, County Donegal. Tombs can be found facing each other and forming a common central court, or back-to-back.

There are other tombs at Malin Moor, County Donegal. Here there are two galleries facing an enclosed court and also two small separate chambers set into the eastern side of the cairn. Remains of pottery were found in the tombs, notably the undecorated Western Neolithic bowls of the type found out Lyles Hill and Donegore Hill.

On farmsteads at Ballynagilly, County Tyrone, a considerable number of later Neolithic decorated bowls were found together with hollow scrapers, javelins, arrowheads, polished stone axes and porcellanite.

Polished stone beads have also been found in court tombs.

Court tombs remained in use for a considerable period of time. Radiocarbon dating indicates that the tombs were first erected about 3800 BC, and they were used for perhaps 1,000 years.

When someone died, certain objects were selected by those performing the burial, and they were left with the body within the tomb. These objects are known as grave goods. It might have been believed that they assisted the soul in its passage to the afterlife. Others believe that the grave goods are objects that the dead person used when he was alive. From objects found in tombs, archaeologists in Ulster have reconstructed much of the lives of these people, but they cannot do the same with their beliefs.

The body was left on a stone pavement within the tomb, and the tomb was sealed.

In 1935 Estyn Evans excavated what he called Dooey's Cairn at Ballymacaldrack, County Antrim. Instead of finding various single-chambered tombs, there was a cremation trench filled with ash and the remains of six persons. Dooey's Cairn has similarities with other burial sites in England and Scotland. Evans's excavation raised a number of issues, and this prompted Pat Collins of the Archaeological Survey of Northern Ireland to re-excavate part of the site forty years later. It has now passed into state ownership.

Pat Collins employed radiocarbon dating, well known by 1975. He revealed that the cremation trench had been in use about 3800 BC, and the presence of post-pits suggested that posts were used to support a platform upon which the bodies of the dead were exposed before cremation. The evidence suggests that there were probably two cremation episodes, one of which involved a timber structure.

Cremation was the usual method of disposing of the dead. After cremation, the bones were picked out of the pyre and buried in one of the chambers of a tomb. The discovery of burnt tools suggests that the grave goods were deliberately placed on the pyre.

Tombs at Audleystown and Ballyalton, County Down, show a number of simple burials. There is evidence that these might have been secondary interments, in some cases coming during the later Neolithic.

Animal bones have also been uncovered from a number of tombs – usually in the chambers of the galleries. Remains at Ballyalton are thought to be vestiges of funeral feasts. Other artefacts found in the tombs include pottery (mostly Lyles Hill and other plain ware), forty-six projectile heads, seventy hollow scrapers, fourteen knives, twenty-seven rounded scrapers, two polished stone axes, ten beads and various other flint tools of unknown function.

The tombs with the largest number of burials are the double court tombs of Audleystown, which were excavated in the 1950s by Pat Collins. Over fifty people were buried here in various chambers. In the north-east gallery of this tomb the remains of twenty individuals were found. Families may have been buried in their own chamber, and the tombs served as a memorial. Each tomb may have been for an individual family. Some of the dead seem to have been laid somewhere else until the flesh decomposed. The corpse had been exposed to the elements before being buried in a tomb.

In Britain the dead were sometimes buried in wooden tombs – a practice that was also known among the Indians of North America.

Humphrey Case has suggested that court tombs were not meant only as tombs. There is evidence of secondary burials in some. Case argued that the type of earth and settlement debris found under the Lyles Hill cairn and on the Goodland site can also be found in the chambers of court tombs. This seems to suggest that court tombs were not built as burial places. Most archaeologists might agree that court tombs were constructed to provide a small setting for special rituals, and the depositing of human remains in the chamber may have been a widespread folk custom. Probably the deceased was an important personage.

It is useful to speculate why there were sometimes multiple chambers. At Audleystown not all chambers appear to have contained human remains. At Creggandevesky, County Tyrone, human remains were found at the entrance to the tomb. Oliver Davies has suggested that bodies were placed in the first chamber and at the entrance, as in Egypt. However, there are a number of tombs where burials had taken place in an inner chamber and not in an outer chamber.

During the Neolithic some tombs seem to have been cleared of their contents. At Ballyreagh, County Tyrone, Oliver Davies found that a tomb had been turned into a pigsty. This poses an intriguing problem: nearly half the chambers with grave goods lack any evidence of human burials.

Court tombs originated in Scandinavia. Ruaidhri de Valera has taken up what archaeologists call the Western Entry Theory. The earliest court tombs, he claims, have been found in the west of Ireland, in the areas of counties Sligo, Mayo and South Donegal. These tombs perhaps represent a colonization of Ireland by farmers arriving from the Continent – perhaps from Brittany. There are several lines of argument about the colonization. It has been suggested that colonization began in the west, where court tombs are clustered most densely, and the largest and most elaborate tombs were later built in the east. The tombs have an east-west orientation and the double-chambered tombs are best preserved in the west. De Valera claimed that farmers from the Continent set up their houses in the west. They then spread eastwards and northwards across the island. The tombs became more scattered across the landscape and they started to deviate from the type of burials which are found in the west. De Valera pointed out that the court tombs in Ulster are similar to some of the early megalithic tombs in Brittany.

On the other hand, a lot of archaeologists have argued that court tombs first appeared on the east coast of Ulster. They find it hard to believe that Neolithic colonists appeared from the Continent and sailed all around the coast of Ireland to establish settlements in the west. Oliver Davies has argued that the court tombs originally had three chambers and that they degenerated into double-chambered tombs – the reverse of what de Valera had argued. It has also been suggested that the origin of court tombs in Ulster lies in the Severn-Cotswold tombs of Southern Britain. They argue that colonists travelled up the Irish Sea, spreading ideas to the east coast of Ulster and the west coast of Scotland.

Since court tombs may have existed for several centuries, it is hard to trace them from a single point of origin. Regional variations may have developed over a period of time. Archaeologists are now more interested in their social function.

The simplest type of court tomb that springs to mind is the portal tomb, or the portal dolmen as it is also known. These tombs have a single chamber built from orthostats. The largest of these tombs have stones standing at either side of the entrance. The term 'door-like' is used to characterize these stones. These tombs are truly spectacular. Cairns originally covered these tombs, and their remains show that they tended to be elongated like the covering of court tombs. That are 174 portal tombs known in Ireland.

Like court tombs, portal tombs were built in a variety of forms. The plan of portal tombs, like those that can be seen at Ballyshannon, County Donegal, or at Sliddery Ford, County Down, is quite simple. However, there are also tombs that look like a cross between a portal tomb and a court tomb. A good example of this is at Ticloy, County Antrim – a single chamber-like portal tomb with a facade of the type more usually associated with court tombs.

The portal tombs are more at the mercy of the elements that court tombs. Excavation has provided much knowledge about court tombs. A rich tomb has been found at Ballykeel, County Armagh. This has yielded a number of decorated bowls and flint tools. The acidic Ulster soils show no evidence that anyone was buried here. At other sites traces of inhumations have been found.

A look at the distribution of portal tombs reveals that they are mainly situated in the north of Ireland. Both portal and court tombs are usually found in the east. They have similar grave goods inside them, such as similarly shaped tools. The portal tomb at Ticloy was almost a miniature court tomb, which prompts the question, which type of tomb was the earliest?

Archaeologists have stated that simple court tombs probably came first. Large tombs with many chambers and ceremonial facades are perhaps features of a later date. Later still, the elaborate facades were abandoned and the number of chambers reduced to one. Portal tombs may be seen as degenerate court tombs.

Others have argued that the evolution of tombs was the reverse of this: that the smaller, most basic tombs must be the earliest. Later on, so it is said, ceremonies for the burial of the dead became more elaborate and new features were added. Eventually the chambers were built as big as an average-sized room. According to this theory, portal tombs may be seen as degenerate court tombs.

Others have argued that the earliest tombs were box-like structures. The ritual involved in the burial of the dead became more elaborate and new features were added, including more-elaborate facades at the entrance of the tombs.

A simple type of Western Neolithic ware has been found in some of the portal tombs, such as Clontygora Small Cairn, County Armagh. Later Neolithic decorated pottery has also been found in such tombs. The evolution of these monuments may have overlapped. Few dispute the fact that their builders and the societies they represented are related.

Undoubtedly, the most notable tombs that come down to us are Neolithic passage tombs. They are found not only in Ireland but also in Western Wales and Scotland – especially in the Orkney Islands. They are also well known in Iberia, Brittany and Southern Scandinavia. There are 229 passage tombs known in Ireland, over half of which are located in five great cemeteries, such as those found in the Boyne Valley, County Meath, and Carrowmore, County Sligo. Passage tombs, however, are not uncommon in Ulster. The largest is at Croaghan/Kilmonaster, County Donegal, where about twelve tombs have been recorded. However, almost all of them were destroyed when they were 'excavated' around 1840.

The main characteristic of a passage tomb is a passage that leads from outside the tomb into the central burial chamber, which may be divided into two or more smaller chambers. A stone cairn covers the tomb. Passage tombs tend to be circular. The cairns are held in place by a surrounding ring of stones, known as kerbstones. There are considerable numbers of megaliths without passage tombs, both in Ulster and Sligo (in the Irish Republic). These have often been referred to as 'simple passage tombs'.

The type of pottery found in passage tombs is known as Carrowkeel ware, taking its name from a passage tomb in County Sligo. Carrowkeel ware is poorly made but well decorated, with deep grooves made with the end of a stick or bird bone. In the more elaborate tombs archaeologists have uncovered pins of antler, pendants and flint tools. Some of the cemeteries also include artwork, usually found decorating the orthostats of the tombs.

An Irish passage tomb that comes to mind is New Grange in the valley of the River Boyne. The equally spectacular tomb at Knowth is surrounded by seventeen smaller tombs. New Grange was covered by a mound that measured 80 metres wide and 11 metres high. Entrance to the tomb was by a long passage formed from orthostats that had also been decorated in the Neolithic period. There are spiral, circular and other motifs. At the end of the passage is a central chamber with a corbelled roof and three smaller chambers. On a large stone those to be cremated were perhaps laid to rest. At New Grange a roof box above the entrance permitted sunlight to cast its beam across the centre of the passage in the main chamber at mid-winter sunrise.

There is nothing so spectacular in Ulster.

The majority of the passage tombs in Ulster are unexcavated, some have been destroyed and a lot have been identified as passage tombs on the basis of descriptions preserved in the Ordnance Survey Memoir of the 1830s. Amongst the more well-known tombs in Ulster is one situated on the top of Slieve Gullion, County Armagh. Here one can see the typical round shape of the mound, the passage and the main chamber. Unlike many passage tombs, the walls here are not constructed out of orthostats, but out of the type of dry-stone walling that a farmer might use to build a field wall.

The tomb was robbed some years before Pat Collins and Basil Wilson could excavate it. All that was left were a few pieces of burnt stone from a circular burial, three basic stones, an arrowhead and some pieces of flint and chert. The tomb is on a high mountain, and this is by no means rare in Ulster.

Other passage tombs have been found at Slieve Donard and Slieve Croob, County Down. At Knockmany, County Tyrone, a single passage tomb was excavated and cremated bones, some flints and a sherd of pottery were found. In Tyrone there is another passage tomb, Sess Kilgreen, and this is perhaps the most ornamented tomb in Ulster. It is decorated with spirals and lozenges. There are no known passage tombs in counties Cavan or Monaghan and only a few in County Fermanagh.

In North Donegal Neolithic (or maybe early Bronze Age) rock engravings have been discovered.

The origin of the passage tombs in Ireland is hotly disputed. Michael Herity of University College Dublin has said that passage tombs were introduced into Ireland by colonists from Brittany. He has argued that these colonists arrived in the region of the River Boyne. From here they gradually spread to the west and north into Ulster. The Boyne tombs, with their passage graves, can be regarded as relics of the earliest colonists.

There are ten simple passage tombs in County Antrim, such as the David Stone at Ballintoy and tomb of the Giant's Ring near Belfast. These are all degenerate tombs.

The Swedish excavator Göran Burenhult and others have argued that the tombs of Carrowmore in County Sligo evolved in the opposite direction – the earliest are the simple ones and the latest are the more elaborate Boyne tombs. There is some radiocarbon and stratigraphic evidence to support this view. At Knowth, one of the three great Boyne tombs, simple passage tombs precede the construction of the larger central tombs. Alison Sheridan has argued that there was a detailed six-squared sequence of passage tombs, which means that the earliest in Ireland are found in Sligo and Antrim. These sites are close to the coast, and it is not possible to know whether they originated from France or Southern Britain. It cannot be discovered why the earliest tombs appear in two such distant areas.

The last type of Megalithic tomb is called a wedge tomb, after its wedge-like shape. That is, the tomb narrows at its far end. These have a single gallery for burials and a short antechamber, which was probably blocked by a stone slab. The burial chamber was probably roofed over with flint slabs. Around the entire gallery is a wall of stone, which retains the cairn. Unlike other tombs, wedge tombs are situated in the south and west rather than the east. There are 465 wedge tombs known in Ireland. These constitute the largest single type of megalithic tomb, though the number in Ulster is not great. Here they are mainly situated in Donegal, Tyrone and Londonderry. Some wedge tombs have also been found in Antrim. Only twenty of these structures have been excavated. Their dates and origin are still much disputed.

In Ulster there is a good wedge tomb at Cloughnagalla, County

Londonderry. Here is found the classic gallery, which is divided from an antechamber by several stones. Kerbstones define the outer boundary of the tomb. Tools, such as flint scrapers and a polished stone axe, have been uncovered. Examination of cremated remains reveals that the individual was an adult female. Cloughnagalla means 'the stone of the hag'.

Flint wedge tombs have yielded remains which can be dated to the start of the Bronze Age. At Loughash, County Tyrone, Oliver Davies discovered a mould for casting a bronze axe, a bronze blade and early Bronze Age pottery, and there is evidence that the tombs themselves were erected during this period.

Like other tombs, wedge tombs have a similar structure to those on the Continent. De Valera has argued that French colonists came ashore at Cork and Kinsale, from where they spread their new tombs northwards through most of the island. Arthur Simon has indicated that he might support the connection with the French tombs, but it is difficult to say whether or not we are dealing with new immigrants. Many archaeologists today point to the possibility that new ideas moved from the Continent or Britain to Ulster, rather than new colonists. One might argue that there is enough similarity between the megalithic tombs and the earlier type to bring about a local development.

Other stone monuments were erected during the megalithic period and into the early Bronze Age. One of the most impressive are stone circles, of which there are about 900 in the British Isles. In Ireland there are two main concentrations of these circles: one in the province of Munster and the other in Central Ulster. Some of the stone circles are found outside these clusters. There are about 100 stone circles in Ulster. In the east of Ulster, stone circles are rare.

The rings of stone include recumbent stones. Over half of the circles had more that twenty stones. Their diameters range from 35 metres in County Tyrone and 33 metres at Ballynoe, County Down to 3.7 metres at Ballybriest, County Londonderry. None are as spectacular as Stonehenge. Very few are more than half a metre in height. However, all stones in each ring are of roughly uniform height. It has been suggested that they were aligned with the rising and setting sun, but a careful examination of these stone circles has not yet revealed any particular alignment.

The dating of the stone circles is also uncertain. Some of them may have been erected during the Neolithic. At Culbane, County Londonderry, a circle of flint implements was discovered in one of the stone circles, and these can be dated to the Neolithic. Artefacts found near stone circles have been used to give approximate dates for their construction. Usually the remains can be dated to the later Neolithic or Bronze Age.

One of the most striking Ulster stone circles lies outside the Central Ulster cluster. At Ballynoe, County Down, the first excavations were in 1937 and 1938 by the famous Dutch archaeologist A. E. van Giffen, who died before his findings could be published. He revealed an extremely complicated monument. At Ballynoe, a large stone circle enclosed a smaller oval of stone and a cairn with chambers at both ends. The presence of a cairn is not unusual. Stone circles throughout Britain have yielded evidence of burials. The Ballynoe circle has so far defied an attempt at reconstruction. Building appears to have been carried out here over a long period of time, beginning in the Neolithic and continuing into the early Bronze Age. Aubrey Burl has noted that a number of the features of the Ballynoe circle – its north-south alignment and its outlying stones – are clearly paralleled in Cumbria in England.

There is another spectacular site at Millin Bay on the Ards Peninsula in County Down. Here Pat Collins and Dudley Waterman excavated another dry-stone wall several feet high. Opposite the construction is a stone cist nearly 6 metres long and less than a metre wide, which contained the remains of at least eighteen people. The bones had been arranged in an orderly fashion. A series of flat stones enclosed the long cist. Many of these had been decorated with patterns, like those found on passage tombs. The remains of Carrowkeel bowls, typical of passage tombs, were found nearby. Beyond the central ceiling was another oval enclosure of upright stones. Other sites remain to be uncovered.

The dead may have been placed in a mortuary house or exposed to the elements until the flesh had decomposed before being placed within a tomb. This practice is also known with the court tombs.

The decoration perhaps emphasizes the importance of these structures, where the remains of ancestors were interred.

Let us now examine henges. A henge is a large circular enclosure with one or more entrances. Sometimes an earthen bank with a ditch on the inside is all that remains. Henges are known throughout Britain and Ireland, but the number excavated in Ireland is small. They appear to be ceremonial enclosures erected at the end of the Neolithic period. It has been suggested that British henges stood in the same relationship to the stone circles as cathedrals stand to smaller churches.

There are few sites in Ulster where henges are found. Dun Ruadh, County Tyrone, may have had a henge where a bank and inner ditch appear to have been built on the site of an earlier Neolithic settlement. Here there is also a large cairn and a number of early Bronze Age burials.

The Giant's Ring near Belfast is a magnificent monument. It consists of an earthen bank about 200 metres in diameter and about 4 metres high. The bank was formed by scraping earth up from inside the ring. Towards the centre of the ring is a small megalithic tomb – perhaps a partly destroyed passage tomb. The tomb was excavated many years ago, but it was also plundered (porter and lemonade bottles have been found 1.2 metres below the tomb). There were traces of burnt bones around the tomb, though nothing of any note associated with the earthen bank. A section through the bank was cut by Pat Collins, who recovered evidence that it had been scraped up from inside the ring. Archaeologists believe that the tomb was of an earlier construction. The circular earthen bank is similar to that of the classic henge monuments, which were already established in Southern Britain and tend to date from the Neolithic or early Bronze Age.

Barrie Hartwell of Queen's University has revealed several new findings concerning this monument. It appears that the hill upon which the monument stands is not big enough for a Neolithic structure. It was hard to make use of a full circle. They had to continually adjust its position in line with the hilltop. Aerial photography has revealed that the Giant's Ring is not alone. There seem to be traces of other circular enclosures in its immediate vicinity. Here there may have been a sizeable rural complex. In the nineteenth century the remains of a number of individuals were recovered from fields near the monument. All this evidence points to the widely held theory that henge monuments were major ritual and social centres. The Giant's Ring is situated near one of the few fords over the River Lagan. It may have served as an important tribal centre for those occupying South Antrim and North Down at the end of the Neolithic.

Before examining the nature of society in Ulster during the Neolithic we must ask whether there was such a thing as 'Neolithic Ulster'. There is certainly an abundance of evidence for Neolithic occupation of Ulster, but it is unlikely that there was a province or kingdom in the north.

It is assumed that the megalithic tombs were the most distinctive ethnic markers at the time. We can be sure that there are no tombs found exclusively in Ulster, so it is hard to talk in terms of a northern kingdom. As the peculiarities of some of the tombs are examined we note that Donegal tombs can be compared with those of Sligo and the rest of Ulster. The court tombs of South Down and Armagh are mainly confined to the Carlingford region. A closer look at the court tombs show that within Ulster there is not the same concentration as there is in the rest of Ireland. For example, court tombs with four or more chambers are mostly confined to the east of Ulster, whilst other court tombs are a phenomenon of the west of the province. The earliest passage tombs are confined to North and East Antrim. The Goodland bowls tend to be confined to the east of Ulster. Thus it is possible to talk of a region within the province or across the borders of Ulster, but there is no indication of an Ulster sphere, kingdom or province.

Evidence of how society was organized in the Neolithic has come down to us: we can estimate the degree to which society was organized by judging the labour required to construct the early settlements and ritual sites that have so far been examined.

D. W. A. Startin has estimated that a Neolithic house, such as that of Ballynagilly, took 550 man hours to construct. It is not known how many field systems were built in Ulster during the Neolithic, but the labour involved was substantial. Seamus Caulfield has suggested that as much labour went into the field systems of North Mayo as went into the construction of the great passage tombs of the Boyne Valley.

The remains of farmsteads at Lyles Hill and Donegore provide us with evidence of Neolithic settlement and engineering in the province. The camps of Southern Britain are open to the same type of analysis.

Was the Donegore site a village? How much effort was put into the construction? How was the labour organized? One of the ditches excavated at Donegore is very similar to that of the British causewayed camps. The ditches were not excavated continuously, but rather in segments, and the segments are of different widths and depths. This suggests that they were excavated at different times, maybe by different work groups. Experiments with an antler pick show that it would have required 18,000 man hours to excavate the two ditches. A population of about thirty people could have built them over several seasons. Not more than five or six families lived within the enclosure, and the workforce would have come from these families. These figures are of course hypothetical. Many teams working at Donegore on different occasions dealt with the workload. Each segment of ditch represents a different team or period of construction. The workforce may have been divided into those breaking up the ground with pickaxes, shovellers and basket carriers for maximum efficiency.

Megalithic tombs like those found in the Boyne Valley are substantial monuments. They were probably erected towards the end of the Neolithic. Construction of the Giant's Ring involved the extraction and piling-up of something in the order of 30,000 cubic metres of soil, entailing about 50,000 to 70,000 man hours. It must have involved the employment of many of the inhabitants for miles around. Large-scale labour is well documented in Southern England, where Colin Renfrew saw how the earlier Neolithic ditched enclosures at length gave way to large henge monuments. What is remarkable about the Giant's Ring is that it is a very large henge existing in a landscape that seems not to have known earlier colonists.

Evidence from the henges points to a society that was probably made up of small families, working together to construct field walls and ditch enclosures. Eventually some areas, like that of the Lower Lagan, saw the appearance of social entities large enough to erect large ceremonial enclosures.

In trying to understand these earlier settlements, a look at the distribution of megalithic tombs is useful. Court tombs are distributed mainly over the northern part of Ireland. They are generally situated on good soil. Evidence for Neolithic settlement is meagre, but archaeologists assume that Neolithic settlements did exist in the area of the tombs. Neolithic farmers, it is speculated, may have been dispersed throughout the Ulster landscape, in a pattern not too different from today's.

Tim Darvill found that court tombs were densely distributed through the island, and they are spaced at an average of about 4.5 km from one another. This spacing of tombs suggests different groups, each having its own territory. These court tombs vary in size. There is no evidence of a hierarchy of settlement, which might suggest that some court tombs were more important than others. According to Darvill, it is possible to identify court-tomb builders as members of segmentary societies.

The segmentary society is a form of social organization well explored by anthropologists, especially in Africa. They tend to be small, numbering fifty to 500 people, and each group is independent, economically and politically, from its neighbours.

Darvill thought that the court tombs served as sites for small groups. In the rural Ulster of today some churches appear to be standing in the middle of nowhere, but they serve the spiritual and social needs of the farms dispersed about them.

The architecture of the court tombs indicates the type of society that built them. Some claim that the court tombs, with their multiple chambers, mirrored in stone the segmented nature of Neolithic society. The galleries are often divided up into individual segments or chambers. When two-, three- or four-chambered galleries occur, they may represent the number of family groups that made up the Neolithic community and built the tombs. It is assumed that court areas were formed for theatrical or ritual performances, which the entire community might attend. The grave goods – pottery, and flint tools – are the same types of artefacts as are found at settlements, and they are perhaps gifts from members of the dead person's family.

The dead include adults and children of both sexes. If everyone belonged to a court-tomb society, it is difficult to understand what happened to the remains of those who were not buried within the tombs. Most Ulster court tombs average only two or three burials, with the exceptions of Audleystown and Creggandevesky. Some think that only important people were buried in the tombs, but there is little evidence to point to this. At Aghanglack, County Fermanagh, a double court tomb has yielded two burials – a child and a juvenile. Our knowledge of Neolithic social structures hardly presupposes the existence of young royalty. There was tomb-robbing, and the acidic soils are capable of completely dissolving bodies over time. Ten or twenty people could have been buried in each tomb, and there were perhaps more tombs than there are today. There is evidence that not more than several hundred people occupied Ulster over a period of centuries, but not all people in the court-tomb societies were interred in the tombs.

Perhaps the majority of the Ulster Neolithic population was not buried in megaliths. On a number of occasions Neolithic burials have been recovered from small pits. Estyn Evans investigated two pits in a gravel quarry at Killaghy, County Armagh, which yielded cremated bones and Neolithic pottery. Brian Williams of the Archaeological Survey of Northern Ireland uncovered four simple pit burials at Altanagh, County Tyrone, which he described as Neolithic. There are very few early Neolithic megatombs known in the province of Munster, but there is increasing evidence that Munster was settled by the Neolithic. This points to the fact that there was a substantial population in Ireland which did not use megalithic tombs for their burials.

Darvill examined the passage tombs and argued that the early segmentary society later changed. Evidence was found that conflicted with the idea of a segmentary society. These tombs are part of the great passage-tomb tradition, which was also seen on the Continent, and may imply the performance of rituals in the region. Passage tombs were mainly for burial, but Darvill states that court tombs were not erected primarily for burial but as the focus of ritual sites. Anthropologists have pointed out that tombs tend to be built on the borders of territories, rather than at their centre. Important tombs probably attracted greater activity, and greater activity led to larger cemeteries. This may well have been the case with the passage-tomb builders, since full cemeteries of passage tombs can be found. These cemeteries are situated at an average of 10.4 km from one another. Dense clusters of tombs in large cemeteries occur in the Boyne Valley and Carrowmore. This seems to point to centres of population as symbols of political importance. There were no large autonomous farming communities scattered across the countryside; rather there were hierarchies in some areas, where people of high status were able to call upon the combined workforce of the countryside.

Unlike court tombs, passage tombs have no open court area for people to witness ritual displays. Ceremonies may instead have been performed within the tombs, where people could assemble after passing through the long, narrow entrance. Some members of society might have been excluded from rituals, which would probably be in the hands of priests. This might be expected in a complex society. The grave goods encountered in many of these passage tombs – stone bells, large antler bones, an abundance of megalithic art, and the long stone basins – speak of esoteric rituals. Rituals and ceremonial practices may have evolved around the passage tombs.

Society in Ireland was becoming more complex by the time of the passage tombs of the Boyne. Alison Sheridan has argued that larger and more elaborate tombs may have been the consequence of competition between different passage-tomb societies. Each tried to display its superiority by building more-elaborate tombs. With the erection of the bigger tombs, like New Grange and Knowth, the competition seems to have collapsed.

There are different types of development between the north and south of Ireland. According to Sheridan, the majority of the Ulster passage tombs belonged to the wealthy. Only eight tombs have been attributed to more developed periods. The passage tombs reflect the evolution of Ulster. There is a dearth of detail about them. Different kinds of tombs could have been built at the same time –

radiocarbon dating is not yet clear. The court tombs probably began earlier, but there seems to be considerable overlap in the times of construction of court, portal and passage tombs.

If court and passage tombs existed at the same time, did they represent two different religions in Ulster in the Neolithic? Perhaps Neolithic settlement in Ulster was not so large as to encourage the organization of labour-intensive projects.

It is not possible to reconstruct life in Ulster during the Neolithic, but individual farms appear to have been part of a greater community. There is evidence for distant exchange systems and a flow of ideas from the Continent and Britain as well as into Ireland. The Neolithic colonists introduced the concept of wealth and status. It is possible that the stone mace heads and large porcellanite axes were at the heart of some kind of exchange economy. There was the phenomenon of individual wealth, and it may have been commercial wealth. The Giant's Ring, standing at the edge of the Neolithic, symbolizes the movement of families of greater social status.

Chapter 4

The Use of Metal

In 1836, Christian Thomsen compiled a guide to the artefacts in the National Museum of Denmark in Copenhagen. He arranged the various finds into three ages: stone, bronze and iron. It became increasingly clear that this was the order of development in Europe and Asia, but in 1857 the Reverend James O'Laverty (among others) argued that such a scheme was inapplicable to Ireland. Along the River Bann in Ulster, near Portglenone, stone and bronze implements were found dating from the same period. Bronze daggers and spearheads found their way to the banks of the River Bann.

As we have seen, the earliest tools in Ulster, during the Mesolithic and Neolithic, were fashioned out of stone. This was followed by a period during which metal tools and weapons were added to the Stone Age technology. They may have replaced most Stone Age tools altogether. Copper was the earliest metal out of which these implements were fashioned, but copper is not generally found in its metallic form. It has to be extracted from rock by heating. The people in Ulster learnt to melt the copper from the ore and pour it into a mould rather than beat it into shape. The addition of a small amount of tin to the molten copper produced bronze – a metal that is much harder and more robust than copper on its own. With the making of bronze tools, weapons and ornaments, the Bronze Age began.

The Bronze Age in Ulster lasted from about 2500 BC to 300 BC, and during this period there was a gradual development of wealth in society. Wealth was displayed in public by those who had the power and prestige to obtain ornaments, weapons and tools of bronze or gold. It is uncertain to what degree the population had access to bronze and gold, for these are quite rare materials and they frequently had to be transported over long distances. Some tools, such as axes, have been widely found, while other artefacts of bronze and gold may have been less widely available and were most likely to be possessed by the chiefs of the community and their families. The Irish annals give a hint of this process when they record that gold-working was taking place in Ulster in the year 1544 BC.

The different classes of society were indicated by the way they dressed. The Bronze Age was therefore a period in which many archaeologists recognize not only a shift from stone to bronze tools but also a revolution in society. The wealthier elements in society used their wealth to emphasize their status, and, in so doing, a social revolution developed.

In Ulster the Bronze Age started at about 2500 BC to 2000 BC, at a time when a type of pot called a beaker started to appear over much of the Continent. The beaker is shaped like a drinking vessel without any handles. Beakers differ from region to region, but they are remarkably simple in shape and ornamentation.

They are generally of better quality than pots made at the end of the Neolithic. On the Continent and in Britain, beakers are normally found in graves along with other items, such as bow strings, flint arrowheads, bones in the shape of bows, and ornaments and small tools of copper, gold and bronze. Beaker burials have been found over much of Western and Central Europe. They can be seen in Hungary and Czechoslovakia, as far north as Scandinavia and as far south as Sicily.

The westernmost place where beakers occur is of course Ireland. The majority have been found in Ulster but there are also clusters of finds in County Dublin and County Limerick. What does this mean? The distribution of finds indicates that people travelled widely, and Beaker folk migrated from the Continent to Britain and Ireland at the start of the Bronze Age. However, some archaeologists do not accept that beakers spread as the result of a single movement of a tribe. They argue that the beaker is the only artefact that unites these areas, and we should not confuse the spread of a pot with the spread of a tribe or people. But beakers were only for the wealthier classes, who were buried with their pots along with other articles. The beakers themselves, it is argued, had a special role in ritual. There are parallels for all this in the later prehistory of Europe and Ireland. For example, wealthier members of communities were often buried with special servings of wine imported from the Mediterranean.

The earliest beakers in Western Europe have been found in Holland, and from there they spread to the British Isles. Archaeologists think that Beaker folk may have entered Ireland by many different routes. There may have been direct contact between Ireland and the rest of Europe, and that may account for the beakers in Limerick or even Dalkey Island, County Dublin. The concentration of beakers in Ulster, especially along the north coast, suggests that they entered Ulster from Scotland. It is difficult to ascertain if these were brought by new people. The existence of substantial Beaker settlements in the Western Isles of Scotland indicates that there was some movement of people.

Evidence of Beaker settlements in Ireland is poor. There are, however, some traces of Beaker huts at New Grange and Knowth, County Meath. There are also Beaker structures at Lough Gur, County Limerick. At Ballynagilly, County Tyrone, the site of a Neolithic house is also the scene of later Beaker occupation. Traces of Beaker pottery have been found. Tools, charcoal-filled pits and ovens occupied 600 square metres. The site dates from about 2500 BC to 2200 BC.

The bog surrounding Ballynagilly provides us with a hint of what happened to the landscape during the early Bronze Age. The forests were cleared by the first colonists, but they later grew back on the site. In the early Bronze Age, the forests were again cleared, so the Beaker settlers at Ballynagilly were farmers, like their Neolithic predecessors. It is known that the people who used beakers grew wheat and barley, and raised cattle, sheep and pigs. At New Grange, County Meath, archaeologists have uncovered evidence that it was the Beaker folk that first introduced horses into Ireland. Apart from Ballynagilly, there are traces of Beaker settlements in the sand hills of

White Park Bay, County Antrim, and at Murlough Bay (Dundrum), County Down. The earliest known Neolithic hearths are at Gortcorbies, County Londonderry. There are also Beaker remains in the Neolithic settlement at the Madman's Window, on the Antrim coast. There is also a Bronze Age settlement at Bay Farm, County Antrim.

Evidence of Beaker burials is rare in Ulster. On the Continent and in Southern Britain those depositing beakers in their graves built their own tombs, but in Ireland the custom of Western Scotland was followed, and Beaker burials took place in earlier monuments. A good example of this was uncovered at Wine Glass Spring, Larganten, County Londonderry, where two tombs were excavated in the late 1930s. The remains of several Beaker folk were discovered in a wedge tomb. Some say that the wedge tombs were erected in the Beaker period, while others have suggested that they were from an earlier period, perhaps the late Neolithic. This is possible. We know that these tombs were used over a long period, and Bronze Age materials have been found within. The Larganten tomb, for example, also contained large items of funerary pottery – food vessels and cordoned urns.

At another wedge tomb, at Loughash, County Tyrone, Oliver Davies uncovered a mould and bronze axes. Once the tombs were erected, the people regarded them as sacred structures, and many generations later they were still used for burials. People were burying their dead in the ruins of old chambers in rural Ireland for some time.

The Beaker folk are better known for their technology rather than for their settlements and burials. An archer's kit made up of barbed arrowheads and stone points is typical of the Beaker period. In Ulster unique arrowheads and bracers have been found in County Antrim. Beaker pottery is also found on the North Antrim coast and along the River Foyle in County Londonderry.

The relationship between Beaker people and the earliest metallurgy in Ireland is debatable. It has been suggested that metallurgy entered Ireland by way of the Beaker folk, by immigration, by direct trading contacts with Iberia or Brittany, or by way of trade with Britain. Many possible sources have been identified. Copper axes have been found in Munster in South-West Ireland where there is the least decay of beakers. In Ulster, where Beaker material is more widespread, it is found that there are scant traces of copper axes. Sources of copper are more abundant in Munster than in Ulster. In the south of Ireland there is evidence of Bronze Age copper mines. However, Ulster has some copper, and that was exploited by early metallurgists.

The beaker is the earliest type of Bronze Age pot, but they are not found in any quantity in Ulster.

After the Beaker period, a number of different ceramic styles appeared in the years from about 2000 BC to 1400 BC. These new pots are divided into a number of different types, but they have several things in common. They are not usually found in settlements but are much more likely to be found in graves. Therefore they are regarded as a special type of funerary ware. They sometimes occur in megalithic tombs that were probably erected in the Bronze Age. Sometimes the grave walls dominate the structure, but often we find instead a well-prepared grave where tombs are made in the form of a stone box. Archaeologists have discovered such objects in cists, accompanying inhumations, but the vast majority have been found in cremation graves. These new types of pottery are, in form and decoration, closely related to similar wares in Britain. It is not possible to determine whether the pottery accompanied new colonists into Ireland or arrived as the result of trading contacts.

A major type of pottery is known as the food vessel. It owes its name to the theory that the pottery served as containers for food offerings for the dead. Judging by their styles, it is thought that they were a later form of beaker. Food vessels are well decorated and can be divided into two or three basic forms: small round-sided bowls (bowl food vessels or Irish bowls), more angular vessels with a pronounced neck (vase food vessels), and large decorated vessels (food vessel urns).

As well as the food vessels, a variety of other urns can be found. Flowerpot-shaped containers with a collar around the upper half of the vessel have been given the name collared urns. These urns were used as containers for the remains of the dead.

Cordoned urns take their name from the fact that they are divided into various zones or cordons.

Another series of vases and urns belongs to an Hiberno-Scots tradition. There are also small rounded bowls which archaeologists call pygmy cups.

The different types of pots pose a lot of problems for archaeologists. They are not found in the same regions or in the same quantities. Arthur Simpson in his survey of the early Bronze Age notes that some bowl food vessels can be found in about 100 sites across Ulster. More than fifty vase food vessels, on the other hand, appear in regional groups, many of them concentrated in East Donegal, the Foyle Basin and North Down. The food vessel urns are mainly a phenomenon of Eastern Ulster. Over twenty of these have a distinctive relief decoration and are often called encrusted urns. They are usually found in County Antrim and County Down. A few are found west of the River Bann. The Hiberno-Scots series has the most pervasive distribution but approximately forty examples of this ware are confined mostly to County Antrim and County Tyrone.

On the basis of all the evidence, a lot of archaeologists argue that Ulster was colonized by many waves of immigrants from Southern Britain. Each employed different types of pottery for the burial of the dead. This not only speaks of Beaker folk but also Food Vessel folk and Urn folk. Others claim that the different pots are the result of contacts between Ulster and the west coast of Britain throughout the early Bronze Age. They believe that this process has more to do with the exchange of ideas than population movements. Some British archaeologists have claimed that the difference between the various types of pot was social rather than chronological. In Britain, urns are usually second to food vessels; it is suggested that those whose burials are associated with urns were of a lower social status than those whose burials are associated with food vessels. There is not much evidence for this in Ulster, where distinquishing between primary and secondary burials is more difficult. It is, however, safe to say that certain forms are more likely to be found together than otherwise. At Kilskeery, County Tyrone, there is an encrusted urn containing a cup, accompanied by five vase food vessels. On Lyles Hill, Estyn Evans uncovered a bowl food vessel, a food vessel urn and maybe a cordoned urn all together.

A better understanding of this elaborate funerary ware would tell us a lot about life in prehistoric Ulster.

All of these pots indicate the presence of regionalism in the early Bronze Age. We can talk of regional groups within Ulster, but we still do not encounter a political or cultural entity, different from the rest of Ireland.

Although the vast majority of early Bronze Age artefacts come from graves, we have a few hints about how these people actually lived during the period after the Beaker folk. On Coney Island in south-west Lough Neagh, Peter Addyman discovered traces of two rectangular houses, which appear to have been constructed with post supports and sod walls. A hearth was found in one of the houses, and bowl food vessels were found lying about the site. The site was probably a small farmstead dating to the early Bronze Age.

At Downpatrick, on the Meadowlands housing estate, two round houses were erected, one of them measuring over 4 metres in diameter and containing a hearth in the centre. The other house was larger – over 7 metres across. Fragments of cordoned urns were found.

Donegore Hill, the site of a large Neolithic ditch, was occupied again during the early Bronze Age. A stockade was constructed here in about 2000 BC.

Other evidence of settlement comes from the remains of Bronze Age pottery found lying in the sand hills along the Ulster coast. At Magheragallon, near Gweedore, County Donegal, a bowl food vessel was found alongside remains of shellfish, dogs, sheep, oxen, red deer, pigs and horse bones.

Hard evidence is sparse. The early Bronze Age site most often encountered is either a single grave or a small cemetery, presumably situated close to a settlement. The pattern seems to differ somewhat after the early Neolithic. Various writers – for example, William Knowles and Edmund Watson – have observed that early Bronze Age funerary pottery is also found in sandhills, especially in County Antrim. Bronze Age burials were often carried out in the valley bottoms – places which are lacking in earlier megalithic monuments.

Farmers expanded into environments that had previously shown little evidence of exploitation, and a number of reasons can be put forward for this expansion. Population increase may have been one reason. Another is that the exploitation of new territory was made easier by the introduction of the plough. Jonathan Pilcher and Alan Smith observed traces of a secondary clearance of land around Ballynagilly, followed by an increase in heathland. This pattern is confirmed by pollen samples in other parts of Ulster, providing strong evidence about the shaping of the modern Ulster landscape. About 2000 BC blanket bog appeared in the mountainous regions and began its general progress across the landscape. Climate change must have had something to do with it. Palynologists have stressed that the changing landscape could have been a result of the transition from the Neolithic into the Bronze Age. Forest clearance in the upland regions brought about an apparently irreversible degradation of the soil. Bog spread into many areas that had previously served for cereal-growing, and there was a shift to the best-drained soils of the lowland regions – sands and gravels, where evidence for early Bronze Age burials have been found. Many think that, with the gradual degradation of important areas of cereal cultivation, the early Bronze Age economy relied more and more on stockbreeding from this period onwards. Today the uplands of Ulster are still covered in blanket peat.

Sometimes it is possible to find remains of early Bronze Age burials in early megalithic tombs. A food vessel and horse bones were found in one of the chambers of the Audleystown court tombs. However, most Bronze Age artefacts come from tombs or graves that were built or dug in the Bronze Age. Early Bronze Age cemeteries may have been entirely flat, with not much covering, or within stone cairns surrounded by a ring ditch, as at Urbalreagh, County Antrim. Here Dudley Waterman discovered the remains of an adult and child buried in cordoned urns.

Often the dead were buried in a pit, or stone cist. Stone cists were made to hold a single body, but sometimes we find more, as at Church Bay on Rathlin Island, where five bodies were uncovered in a single cist. Grave goods were limited to one or two pits; many pits contain no pottery. Occasionally metal objects are found in the tombs.

A good example of this is Carrickanab, near Downpatrick, County Down. Here a stone cist contained the remains of one body accompanied by a food vessel, a bronze dagger, a bronze awl and two flint scrapers. Another bronze dagger was found with a bowl buried at Corkey, County Antrim.

At Bay Farm, at Carnlough, County Antrim, a collared urn was discovered. It had been placed upside down near the cremated remains of a body; a bronze dagger was found with the urn, as also was a steel button and a curious piece of chalk.

More burials have been discovered without any burning of the body. At Claudy, County Londonderry, Nick Brannon of the Archaeological Survey of Northern Ireland discovered a young man buried with a food vessel. He was about 1.9 metres (6' 2") tall. His right arm was more developed than his left. It has been suggested that the man had developed his right side in a pursuit such as carpentry.

Burials were not only carried out individually. A number of graveyards are comprised of larger graves, each containing several bodies. One of the largest prehistoric graveyards in Ulster is at Cloughskelt, County Down. Here Laurence Flanagan has uncovered twenty graves with food vessels and encrusted urns. Some bodies were buried in individual pits; others lay within a box-like structure of stones; others had a complete stone cist to themselves. At Terryglass, County Tyrone, eight cist burials were discovered.

An even more extensive graveyard existed at Dun Ruadh, County Tyrone. Here an early cemetery was inserted in what appears to be an earlier henge monument. The graveyard consisted of a large stone cairn, the centre of which included a pear-shaped cobbled area approached through an entrance way. Upright stones and dry-stone walling make up half of the interior of the cairn, which is thought to have been an area of ritual. About a dozen cists, most of which contained food vessels, have been inserted into the cairn. Burials also took place outside the cairn. Derek Simpson discovered an early Bronze Age cremation inserted into the earthern bank of the henge.

The burials tell us some details about life in the early Bronze Age. At Altanagh there are eight burials. Some are in cists; some of the remains were placed in cordoned urns. There were also simple pit burials. The remains of a young female and an elderly male suffering from arthritis were found in one of the cists; a cordoned urn contained the remains of a male of about sixteen to eighteen years old. They were accompanied by bones of pig and cattle – perhaps the remains of a funeral feast.

In another cordoned urn were the remains of a young woman,

twenty-five to thirty years old, who had been buried with her bedding and other objects. Life was not long in this Bronze Age environment; of the bodies found at Altanagh, both Neolithic and Bronze Age, all but two died before the age of thirty-five.

The Bronze Age saw the introduction of metal tools. This was a revolution in technology. A hint of the impact of this change can be obtained if we reflect on the nature of early Bronze Age metalworking. First it was necessary to acquire the necessary metals: copper, tin and gold. The only known Bronze Age mine in Ireland was at Mount Gabriel, County Cork. There were probably others. As far as it is known, they had their origins in Cornwall, which is famous for its mines. Gold was found on the island, mainly in County Wicklow, but nearly all the metal known in Ulster originates from outside the province, so metalworking must have involved long-distance trading. The great effort required to obtain raw materials would have made all metals precious to early Bronze Age communities. However, it cannot be absolutely proven that people in Ulster were not exploiting their own natural resources. Copper, for example, might have been obtained from a number of sites, especially in County Tyrone, and tin deposits exist at Slieve-na-Mistkan in the Mourne Mountains. Gold has also been discovered in Ulster in the sands of the River Moyola in the Sperrin Mountains and at Slieve-an-Orra in County Antrim. There is no absolute proof that these deposits were used in Ulster in the prehistoric period.

County Antrim produced more bronze than anywhere else in Ireland. Does this indicate that this was the area with the highest prehistoric population density?

In the nineteenth century, William Arthurs, who loved the Glens of Antrim, searched for artefacts that he might sell to collectors.

Bronze Age smiths cast metal to make tools, weapons and ornaments, and moulds have been uncovered in Ulster. The simplest form of casting involved the use of an open stone in which the shape of the artefact had been cut. When the molten metal was poured into the mould, it set almost immediately. The smith could then remove it and hammer the edges into shape. A sandstone mould for casting axes has been recovered from near Ballynahinch, County Down.

As the Bronze Age progressed, new and more complicated

objects were cast in these simple open moulds; for example, a socketed spearhead was made, which consisted of the spearhead with a hollow socket into which a wooden shaft was set. To make such a weapon, the smith would have employed a two-piece mould, often of soapstone or chlorite schist. Here two corresponding moulds were hollowed out in order to cast both sides of the spearhead, and a small piece of clay would be inserted into the mould to exclude the molten bronze. The clay was later removed to leave a hollow socket for the spear shaft.

In Ireland, tools and weapons made from molten metal show a definite progression from very simple forms to increasingly complex designs. The earliest metal tools in Ireland are copper axes cast from open moulds. Five hundred of these have been excavated in the island, while only about eighty are known in the whole of Britain. The greatest distribution in Ireland lies in Munster, but Ulster has a considerable share. Some archaeologists think that the technology for the manufacture of these axes came to Ulster from the Continent via Southern Ireland. After the initial process of axe-making in copper, smiths adopted the use of bronze and added decorations. Experiments have shown that early Bronze Age axes were about twice as efficient as polished stone axes.

Bronze axes may not always have served as tools. Those that were covered in decoration may have had a similar function to the decorated Malone-type porcellanite axes that Greer Ramsey had observed. They may have been used in ritual combats by the aristocracy. Primitive axe heads wobbled on the end of their wooden shafts. In order to prevent this, the smiths cast and hammered a small flange that made the head more secure.

Other tools and weapons were also improved. As time passed daggers increased in length and tangs and rivets were used to secure the blade firmly to the handle. A dagger with a gold-decorated pommel was found buried at Topped Mountain Cairn, County Fermanagh. It was probably of great value and prestige. As well as the dagger, a golden halberd dating from the early Bronze Age has been found. This weapon is essentially a dagger mounted at right angles on a long pole. In this case the blade was fastened so weakly to the pole that it has been suggested that it served for ritual or display rather than as an actual weapon. The halberd was popular in Ireland.

Flint tools and weapons continued to be used in the early Bronze Age. During the Neolithic, arrowheads were leaf-shaped, but in the early Bronze Age a new type of flint arrowhead is to be found. This called for great craftsmanship. Many such arrowheads have been found – for example, at Ballyclare, County Antrim. The long javelin was confined to the early Bronze Age. By the end of this period in Ireland, smiths were casting metal spearheads with hollow sockets using bivalve moulds.

Other flints that have survived include scrapers, which were not easily replaced. Simple flint knives were also made, and some metal tools, such as awls and chisels, were introduced.

To tools and weapons must be added ornaments of bronze and gold. These include rings and bracelets, small gold discs that may have served as pendants or decoration for clothes, and, finally, the famous Irish lunulae, or 'small moons'. The lunula takes its name from its crescent shape. They were made of gold beaten very thin. Then they were often covered in the same type of ornamentation as we sometimes find on Beaker pottery. They were probably worn about the neck, and they may have been symbolic. Today the president of the Royal Society of Antiquaries of Ireland wears a number of lunulae. About eighty Bronze Age lunulae have been discovered in Ireland; they have also been found in Britain and on the Continent. In Ireland, lunulae have never been discovered during an actual excavation, so it is difficult to be sure of either their actual date or their role in society. Joan Taylor placed the lunulae within the later part of the Beaker period. However, although many graves from this period have been excavated, no lunulae have been discovered among the grave goods. She has suggested that they were never personal property like daggers or pots, but perhaps they were used as a sign of lineage or connected with some form of unknown ritual.

The erection of stone monuments such as circles appears to have begun in the later Neolithic, but the main period of erection seems to have been the early Bronze Age.

The simplest type of monument found in the early Bronze Age would have been a standing stone. This is a simple upright stone, such as those which nowadays might be found in a farmer's field.

Some of these have been excavated to investigate their purpose. At Drumnahare, Loughbrickland, County Down, Pat Collins found cremated human bones at the base of a standing stone. He also excavated a possible Bronze Age burial at the foot of a stone at Carrownacaw, also in County Down. The only other excavated stone is on a housing estate near Dundonald, County Down, but here the only evidence of burial was the recent interment of a dog wrapped in a hessian bag. It also appeared to be the burial site of a pet rabbit. About 50 metres away, however, human remains were found, and they have been dated to the end of the Bronze Age.

Some have suggested that these standing stones were erected as grave markers, for there is some evidence that burials took place at the foot of the stones. It is also possible that they were erected for other reasons. Others have suggested that the stones marked ancient pathways, but it must be admitted that one cannot always see from one stone to the next. The only fact that is certain is that they remain a mystery.

Stone circles started in the Neolithic and continued through until the Bronze Age, but it is a clever archaeologist who can say which circle belongs to which period. The circles seem to demonstrate a degree of continuity between the later Stone Age and the early Bronze Age. Continual change must have taken place, and we must be wary in assuming that these ages were culturally distinct periods in Ulster's prehistory.

The majority of Ulster's stone circles are concentrated in the middle of the province, in County Tyrone, but there are other noteworthy examples, such as Beltany Stone Circle in County Donegal. This circle consisted of about eighty stones, and it was one of the largest circles in the island. The most elaborate system of circles is at Beaghmore, County Tyrone. This consists of three pairs of stone circles, a series of stone alignments, several circular 'rockeries' of upright stones and a dozen small stone cairns, most of which cover a cremation burial. Radiocarbon dating from both sites and the surrounding bog points to occupation in Neolithic times and through to the Bronze Age.

Some archaeologists and astronomers have claimed that the stone circles were laid out in accordance with geometrical principles.

Circles and egg-shaped patterns, such as those found at Beaghmore, were constructed along these lines. Alexander Thom has pointed out that two stones at Beaghmore are aligned with the sun at the summer solstice. The passage tomb at New Grange is aligned to catch the light on the midwinter sunrise. There are therefore three possible functions for the stone circles: burials, public rituals and astronomical observations.

Some archaeologists recognize the division of the Bronze Age into three periods: early, middle and late. It is not too difficult to recognize ware from the early and late Bronze Age, but there is no distinctive pottery known from the period between 1500 BC and 1200 BC other than coarse bucket-shaped pottery, sometimes known as flat-rimmed ware. It is not useful to talk in terms of a distinctly middle Bronze Age type of settlement.

A possible candidate for a middle Bronze Age settlement is a small site excavated by Henry Hodges on the present shore of Cullyhanna Lough, County Armagh. Architectural remains consist of an outer enclosure, about 20 metres across, constructed of upright oak stakes. Within the enclosure were a timber-built hut about 6 metres across with a central hearth, and a semicircular structure that may have served as a windbreak for a hearth. There have been very few finds and nothing that helps towards dating. Henry Hodges has suggested that it may have served as a hunting lodge. There is a comparison between the way of life suggested by the architecture and the literary descriptions of Finn MacCool and his *fianna* bands. They hunted from May through to October. Henry Hodges could only guess at the date of the site. The oak posts that made up the enclosure and the stakes that were used in the construction of the hut were preserved and later examined by the palaeontology laboratory at Queen's University Belfast. Since 1968 researchers such as Mike Baillie, Jonathan Pilcher and Jennifer Hallam have been attempting to establish the technique of tree-dating (dendrochronology) in Ireland. This technique was first developed in the American south-west. However, many thought that trees growing in the wet Irish climate would show insufficient seasonal and yearly variation in growth rates for the technique to be successful here.

A tree such as an oak puts on a ring each year, so one can tell the age of the oak tree by counting the rings. As climate conditions vary from year to year, the width of the growth rings will reflect that variation. By comparing the ring patterns in wood of known and unknown age, it is possible to effect dating.

Tree-ring data at Belfast date back to 5400 BC – one of the most complete records in the world – but when the samples from Cullyhanna Hunting Lodge were obtained in the 1970s dating was uncertain. Ring samples, however, indicated that the stakes used to build the outer enclosure and the hut were taken from trees felled in the same year. Two radiocarbon dates from a single sample can yield different results, so radiocarbon dating can never pinpoint a precise date. For example, one of the dates obtained from Cullyhanna records a 95% chance that the wood comes from between 2030 BC and 1620 BC; the same sample of wood also gave a date between 1740 BC and 1400 BC. Now, with a much more complete record of tree-ring data, we are able to say accurately when the trees that produced the stakes at Cullyhanna were felled: 1526 BC. This places Cullyhanna in the period between the early and so-called middle Bronze Age. This is still the earliest dating of an archaeological site in Ulster using dendrochronology.

Henry Hodges has investigated another site that was possibly contemporary with Cullyhanna. There is much evidence for special outdoor cooking places during the Bronze Age. They are known in archaeological literature as fulachta fian. Wooden troughs were set into the ground and filled partly with water, which was then heated by dropping hot stones into it. It was brought to the boil, and could cook a meal in about four hours. The evidence from some of these cooking places indicates that they were used hundreds of times. Such sites occur in great numbers in the south of Ireland, but they are very rare in Ulster. Henry Hodges excavated one such site at Ballycroghan, County Down, this being the best example of a fulachta fian. Here several cooking places were found, one of which had an oak-lined trough about 2.5 metres long. Near it was a mound of stone and the charcoal remains of the fire used for heating stones. Neither the logs nor the site itself has been dated, but Richard Warner, elsewhere in Ireland, has suggested that the greatest period of fulachta-fian construction may have been during the Bronze Age, up until 1200 BC. There is evidence that they continued to be built all the way into the Middle Ages.

In the middle Bronze Age, tools and weapons were further modified and improved. Axe heads were made with enlarged flanges, which were hammered firmly into position around a wooden shaft. These axes are often called winged, or wing-fangled, axes because of the long flange that gripped the axe head. The problem of the butt of the axe biting further and further into the handle with each blow was solved by hammering ridges into the handle. Smiths created the palstave, a type of chisel, with notable high-flanged sides that fit into a split handle rather than a socket. The palstave is one of the great inventions of the middle Bronze Age. Further improvements came in the late Bronze age.

Greer Ramsey has pointed out that the use of very large axes could also be justified by the scale of the woodworking at this time. Spearheads were reinforced by extending the cavity so that the shaft ran further into the spearhead. This was an improvement on earlier spearheads, which were liable to come out of a rather shallow socket.

The addition of loops for fastening the spearheads more tightly was accompanied by more-elaborate decorations. Loops were of three types, confined to the butt or protected within the blade itself, and they correlate with the size of the weapon. Greer Ramsey has recorded the number of finds in Ireland of each of the three types: about 650 side-looped, 1,500 based-looped, and only about 40 protected-looped. Some of the largest spearheads were used as ceremonial weapons or objects of great prestige. The lightest spears may have been used for thrusting rather than throwing. In Britain similar weapons have been found embedded in the soil.

Early Bronze Age warriors were armed with daggers, and bows and arrows. The dagger was gradually lengthened into larger weapons – dirks and rapiers. These were thrusting weapons, and rapiers are among the most common weapons from the Bronze Age. The most famous rapier was found in a bog at Lissan, County Londonderry. At 80 cm in length, it is the largest rapier in Western Europe.

Greer Ramsey observed that although the Lissan blade was unique in that there were three rivets firmly holding the blade to its shaft, it was difficult to imagine such a weapon used in conflict. This rapier, along with the larger spears and axes, was probably used in ceremonies or parades. The discovery of a large percentage of these middle Bronze Age objects in bogs and rivers raises the question of whether they were used as ritual offerings.

Ramsey has assembled some useful data about where bronze artefacts of the early and middle Bronze Age have been found in Ireland. Axes have generally been recovered from dry-land sites; spears have generally been recovered from bogs and rivers; and dirks and other weapons are also associated with rivers, particularly in the region of the River Bann as a result of drainage operations in the nineteenth century. The River Bann has been cited as a dividing point in Ulster, geographically and politically. Some of the weapons recovered are from battles or were deposited as part of some riverine burial ritual. Today many would argue that they were placed in their final resting places as an act of ritual. Metal objects were offered up to the gods – a practice (as we have seen) peculiar to the early Bronze Age.

Technological changes in the middle Bronze Age indicate improvements in the production and use of metal. Many artefacts were made in Ulster, where there is evidence of local casting. At Killymaddy, County Antrim, there is a whole series of two-piece stone moulds for casting spearheads and dirks. There are also simple razors and even sickles. Bronze razors are well known in Ireland.

Major changes in society probably took place with the inception of metallurgy in Ireland. Objects were fashioned from valuable metals and stratified societies developed. The upper classes displayed their own wealth and prestige by the possession of metal weapons and ornaments. Throughout the early and middle Bronze Age, bronze gradually replaced stone as the main manufacturing material. This change took place not only in Ireland but all over Europe.

Peter Harbison has noted that one of the fundamental differences between the Neolithic and the early Bronze Age was the shift from communal to individual burial. The megalithic tombs provided a repository for at least a small part of the community, but in the early Bronze Age we find individual burials, and grave goods show that a new class was emerging in the province. The majority of Bronze Age graves contain the remains of only one body – and a considerable number of early Bronze Age cemeteries have been studied. Nearly fifty sites have two burials, and at almost forty others the burials are bound together. Twenty per cent of Bronze Age cemeteries have between four and ten graves, and only 10% have more than ten graves. These may have been small family cemeteries, and the paucity of graves may indicate that families stayed only a short time in one place.

Great quantities of grave goods have been discovered in many of the cemeteries. At Ballymacaldrack, County Antrim, examples of fine beach ware were uncovered, and they included a vase food vessel, a food vessel urn and collared urns. The community was adopting new styles at this period of burials. John Waddell has suggested that different communities with different wares were buried there in the same cemetery. He says that the likelihood is that Bronze Age cemeteries had another purpose, apart from burial. They may also have been sacred areas for communal rituals in which a great number of classes took part. A great number of burial sites from the early Bronze Age have come to light, but evidence of burials in Ulster disappears by the middle Bronze Age. Bronze Age funerary wares in Ulster, as in other parts of Ireland, all seem to originate in the early Bronze Age.

Gold lunulae have also been found in Scotland, so we believe exchanges took place between people of considerable social status. A bronze dagger was found at Topped Mountain Cairn, County Fermanagh, and its gold pommel is similar in style to others found in Scotland and the rich burial sites of early Bronze Age Wessex. There were movements of people, and it would still seem improbable that similarities in metal artefacts – particularly grave goods – are merely the result of an exchange of ideas.

The Bronze Age is characterized by the growing production and elaboration of weapons. The new upper classes were concerned with military display and warfare, and this becomes even more evident in the late Bronze Age.

Chapter 5

Warlike Tribes

The late Bronze Age started about 1200 BC, but it is difficult to say exactly when and how it ended. Typically late Bronze Age metalwork has been discovered from as late as 300 BC, several hundred years after the Iron Age metalwork first began. Large Bronze Age developments can be followed to about the third century BC.

The late Bronze Age provides a great wealth of artefacts from Irish prehistory, and museums are filled with impressive quantities of bronze and gold objects. However, very few details of how the people lived or how they buried their dead has survived.

Archaeologists argue that society in Ulster became more stratified than ever before, and there was an increasing emphasis on warfare. This is evident from a study of the settlements and weapons of the period.

During the 1960s and early 1970s Dudley Waterman of the Archaeological Survey of Northern Ireland carried out excavations at Navan Fort, County Armagh, the north's greatest archaeological site. Here there are two monuments within the remains of a large circular earthwork, nearly 290 metres across. The first monument, Site A, is a low mound surrounded by traces of a ditch some 50 metres in diameter. The second monument, Site B, is a much larger mound, of a similar diameter to Site A but standing some 6 metres high. Waterman excavated part of Site A and most of Site B.

On the surface of the Site B he found traces of Neolithic settlement in the form of pottery. He also found a layer of soil that had been ploughed – perhaps in the Bronze Age. The mound was probably built about 800 BC. The circular ditches of Site B formed an enclosure about 45 metres across. The ditches are not steep, only about 1 metre deep, and 5 metres across the top. Inside the circular ditch was a ring of pits, which seem to have served as post-holes for a palisade. The site was entered by a causeway on the eastern side. The purpose of this site is not known, but perhaps it was used for ritual purposes.

Sometime before 100 BC, either at the end of the late Bronze Age, or perhaps in the succeeding Iron Age, the enclosure became a scene of great activity. The people of Navan built a sequence of huts, measuring about 10 to 13 metres across. The huts were built of timber or wattling. It seems that the huts were replaced seven or eight times. Chris Lynn uncovered evidence at an early Christian site – Deer Park Farms, County Antrim – which suggests the wattle-and-daub houses were replaced at intervals of twenty years or less. Near the huts at Navan, a second series of structures, each measuring about 18 to 20 metres across was built. They may have served as courtyards or animal pounds of the type associated with smaller dwellings. A system of dual buildings was replaced by three small circular huts.

Around the entrance area were found the remains of coarse bucket-shaped pottery with some objects of bronze. Other finds include the remains of a sickle or reaping hook and another piece of metal, which may have been part of a spearhead. The hut survived into the Iron Age without any breach in continuity.

Site A, a short distance away, contained more circular buildings. Although there are no definite dates for the structures, they are thought to date from the late Bronze Age and early Iron Age. Navan Fort may have extended beyond the area of the visible monuments, and more buildings may have existed on top of the hill.

The surrounding bank and ditch have been excavated, and this has raised further interesting questions. For example, an outer bank and an inner ditch have been found. They are of a configuration which is typical of late Neolithic henges, and it is the reverse of what may be expected in a hill fort. An outer bank provides an attacker with an opportunity to gain higher ground than the defender. Derek Simpson has suggested that Navan Fort originally served as a henge monument with a long enclosure.

David Weir has also examined the ditch, which was originally 2 or 3 metres deeper than it is today, and, from a pollen core, Weir has obtained evidence that the ditches were built before 400 BC – that is, by the late Bronze Age – but how much earlier they are remains a mystery.

Navan Fort emerges as the Emain Macha of early Irish tradition, and perhaps it was the capital mentioned in the early annals. The enclosure was of considerable size, and this clearly marked it out as a very important site. There are similar enclosures at Knockaulin, County Kildare, which is identified with Dun Ailinne, the ancient capital of Leinster. Perhaps 'royal' sites were being erected throughout Ireland by the late Bronze Age, and perhaps henge-like enclosures were used for ceremonial purposes rather than defensive ones.

Animal remains have been discovered at Navan Fort, so it may have been the scene of feasts. The most common animal remains come from pigs, and this is surprising given that cattle is the favourite beast of early Irish literature. However, pork was the main dish at royal feasts. The skull of a Barbary ape has also been found there. Barbary apes live in North Africa, and they were perhaps shipped up the Atlantic seaways to Ulster. Perhaps this ape was a gift. Animals have always been revered as presents. During the Middle Ages Harun al-Rashid sent the Emperor Charlemagne an elephant. Another tale records that an Icelander presented a gift of an animal to the King of Denmark.

About three quarters of a mile west of Navan Fort lies Haughey's Fort, a late Bronze Age hill fort. It was built and occupied in about 1100 BC. It covers an area about 340 metres in diameter. From the ground there is no visible trace of a ditch, but the location of one can clearly be seen from the air. The ditch measured about 4 metres across at the top and was dug to a depth of about 2.5 metres. It was cut in the shape of a V – a form often employed in defensive ditches of the age. It was too wide to leap, and attackers that tried to climb in and out of the ditch would find themselves in a sticky situation. The steep sides were hard to climb, especially in the wet. Unlike Navan Fort, Haughey's Fort was probably a defensive site.

Most of the inner ditch was waterlogged, and from it remains of animal bones, brushwood and wooden implements have been recovered. The remains include the handle of an object like an axe or pick.

Bones from the largest known cattle in prehistoric Ireland were found here – and remains have been found in many prehistoric sites in the island. The ditch yielded two dog skulls – the largest known from any prehistoric site in the British Isles. The dogs must have been the size of a modern Alsatian, and, as Richard Warner of the Ulster Museum has pointed out, their presence is consistent with the idea that this was a royal site. The aristocracy would be expected to have larger animals than other people. In a tale of *The Ulster Cycle*, 'The Cattle Raid of Cooley', a dispute takes place between the King and Queen of Connaught and the King of Ulster as to who should own the largest bull. This ditch has also yielded eighty species of beetles and enough insects and chemical evidence to suggest that it possibly served as the latrine for the settlement when it wasn't dampening the ferocity of any attackers.

Within the enclosed area a large number of pits were discovered. Here were found cooking pots and the remains of burnt stones, ashes, pottery, bones and barley. The ditch also yielded several saddle querns, which were used in the grinding of grain. Traces of gold-casting were also found. No houses were located, but a long line of post-holes points to the presence of some form of stockade within the site.

Below Haughey's Fort lies a unique archaeological site, known locally as the King's Stables. Tradition has it that the early Kings of Ulster stabled and watered their horses here. In the 1970s Chris Lynn of the Archaeological Survey of Northern Ireland conducted a small excavation on this unique monument. Its radiocarbon suggests that it was contemporary with Haughey's Fort. It was probably built by the occupants of the hill fort. The site is a nearly circular hollow, about 25 metres across and 4 metres deep. Examination showed that it was originally filled with water to this depth. It appears to have been man-made. In the bottom of the pool were discovered the remains of small moulds, animal bones and part of a human skull. The animals included cows, red deer, dogs, pigs and sheep, which are not typical of the food remains of an ordinary settlement. There were very few sheep at that time. An abundance of antlers and dogs, combined with the condition of some of the animals, has led to the conclusion that either the entire animal or part of it was tossed into the water without having been butchered or cooked. The remains of a young mare were also discovered, but the facial part of the skull had been cut away. This may have been a ritual pool, and the animals may have been offerings to the gods. This practice is well documented on the Continent from the late Bronze Age and the Iron Age. The King's Stables is the only known prehistoric pool in the British Isles.

Navan Fort seems to have been a royal site or tribal centre, but it is not certain who the occupants were. It was clearly a major fortified settlement in the province at this time.

Richard Warner has also excavated the remains of the late Bronze Age settlement at Clogher, County Tyrone. The site at a later date was the capital of the Airgialla, the successors of the dynasty that ruled at Navan Fort. Here Bronze Age remains, like those at Navan, are sited on a hilltop. They include traces of structures and coarse-ware pots. The defences appear to have been constructed out of timber and stone. This technique is most often found in Iron Age Celtic forts across Europe.

Another fort was studied by Richard Warner, at Rallagh, County Londonderry, shortly before it was destroyed by quarrying. He believed that the timbers used in its construction were like those found in Scotland in the same period.

Lyles Hill, famous for its Neolithic settlement, also reveals evidence of occupation during the Bronze Age. Its earlier Neolithic neighbour, Donegore Hill, has also shown late Bronze Age occupation in the form of circular structures that measured 8 metres across.

Settlements in Ulster have never been limited to dry-land sites. In the historic period, crannogs (fortified dwellings in a lake or marsh) were constructed in a circular shape. They were made out of brushwood, timber, stone and other materials, enclosed within a ring of timber poles. These structures were for defensive purposes, and perhaps they were the residences of the more powerful members of society. It is not clear what their origins were. Chris Lynn has stated that the defensive nature of the medieval crannogs does not set them apart from earlier lake dwellings, which were seen in the Neolithic, as already stated, at Lough Enagh. By the late Bronze Age there were some very good examples of these settlements in Ulster.

In 1953, the level of Lough Eskragh, County Tyrone, dropped considerably as large quantities of the water were being consumed by a textile mill. The lower water level provided a unique opportunity to investigate and recover much evidence of late Bronze Age people in Ulster. Pat Collins and William Seaby examined several different sites. Twenty years later the level of water dropped again, and Brian Williams had the chance to re-examine the site before it was again inundated.

Structures were revealed along the prehistoric shoreline, and about 15 metres offshore there appears to have been a crannog within the lake itself. The crannog was built by ramming small birch pilings into the bed of the lake. A round platform, about 10 metres across, was built on the pilings out of timber and brushwood. Using dendrochronology, an oak plank from the crannog was dated to the tenth century BC. Another piece of oak was radiocarbon dated to between 920 BC and 790 BC. In the crannog were two coarse-ware pots, along with other fragments of coarse ware, saddle querns and a bracelet. Nearby, Collins and Seaby discovered two dugout canoes. They were hollowed out of oak and measured 7 metres in length. In one of the canoes was a vessel carved from alder. During Brian Williams' examination, another alder vessel was found. Perhaps the canoes and the crannog were contemporary with each other. The alder vessels provide a reminder that a lot of household utensils in the prehistoric period were fashioned out of organic materials, such as wood.

The structure along the shoreline was made up of nearly 600 piles of birch and ash, whose points had been sharpened with bronze axes. Seventeen saddle querns were recovered from this area. A radiocarbon sample from the piles indicated a date between 790 BC and 400 BC. A bronze axe was also recovered.

At a second site, about 120 metres from the first, upright posts and burnt wood were found, but there was an indication of something else too: alongside a large stone pile, which had evidently been buried, were fragments of clay moulds for casting bronze swords. Everything points to this being the workshop of a bronze-smith. Radiocarbon gave a date between 1520 BC and 1140 BC, but this date poses some difficulty. The type of bronze sword being cast on the site should not have appeared before 900 BC.

Further evidence of lakeside settlements have been found at Island MacHugh, County Tyrone. This site was excavated in the 1930s by Oliver Davies. Here he found the remains of a brushwood platform and a quantity of later Bronze Age pottery. Derek Simpson's and Richard Ivens' more recent excavations have recovered evidence that Island MacHugh was occupied between 1200 BC and 800 BC, or much later. Brian Williams has also uncovered evidence of a late Bronze Age lake settlement at Lough MacHugh.

There is of course an abundance of relics from the later Bronze Age, but we cannot assume that every Bronze Age Ulsterman lived behind an earthen bank or on a timber platform surrounded by water. Remains of Bronze Age settlements have been discovered in upland regions, such as at Ballyutoag, County Antrim. Here there was a round house within a stone-built oval enclosure. This was first investigated by Oliver Davies, and radiocarbon dating places it in the late Bronze Age. Coastal settlements persisted through to the late Bronze Age on the North Antrim coast, mainly in the region of White Park Bay. An abundance of coarse-ware pottery has been discovered in the region's sand dunes. Twenty circular huts, about 6 metres in diameter, have been found here, mainly along the shore. They have been attributed to a period from the Neolithic to the late Bronze Age. On a lesser scale, there is evidence of Bronze Age burials at Bay Farm III near Carnlough, County Antrim, and there is also evidence of a late Bronze Age settlement on this exposed coast.

Pollen has been obtained from various Ulster sites, such as

Gortcorbies in County Londonderry, Sluggan and Altnahinch in County Antrim. In every case the pollen tells the same story: between 1200 BC and 1000 BC there was a dramatic decrease in tree pollen as forests were cleared. There were cycles of forest clearance alternating with periods of reforestation. Another period of clearance occurred around 900 BC, when there seems to have been a general pattern of clearance over the landscape for the development of agriculture. Radical changes were taking place concurrently in industry, ornaments, warfare and agriculture.

General trends in the environment may be seen in the pollen record, but it may not be so useful in telling us about sudden changes, long- or short-lived. Archaeologists and physical scientists have been interested in short periods of climate fluctuation that may have struck Ulster during the late Bronze Age. Some suggest that Mount Hekla, a volcano 1,300 km north of Ulster, may have affected life in Ulster for over 3,000 years. Volcanoes such as Mount Hekla throw thousands of tons of dust into the sky, and, amongst other things, this dust severely alters global and local climate. It has been suggested that, during the period which is now being examined, Mount Hekla experienced a major eruption, resulting in a mini version of the dreaded nuclear winter. Dust, by reflecting sunlight, would have reduced warmth in the north of the British Isles and increased rainfall. This would have made the uplands unsuitable for growing crops, and is likely that upland settlements were abandoned. Communities were forced from the uplands. John Baker has suggested that this happened during the late Bronze Age in Scotland. He sites the abandonment of 1,000 late Bronze Age huts in Caithness, and earlier villages in North Uist during the twelfth century BC. This eruption of Mount Hekla has been dated using numerous techniques. As populations moved into lowland areas, competition for land led to increased warfare and the construction of defensive sites. But was this the situation in Ulster?

The question is quite hard to answer, but the answer may lie in dendrochronology. Tree rings provide us with information about climate changes. In extremely wet weather the oaks growing around the edge of a lake are under severe stress and their growth rings become narrow. Mike Baillie of Queen's University has observed that in the period from 1159 BC to 1141 BC the oaks did experience a period of great stress. The narrow tree rings suggest a rising of water level, perhaps brought about by increased rainfall.

These dates fit into the period that other scientists have assigned to the third great Mount Hekla eruption. It also fits in with a period when uplands were abandoned in Scotland, where evidence of Bronze Age settlement is more extensive than it is in Ulster. We can go further still and state that the archaeological records for Ulster fit in with the idea that a similar shift in the population occurred here.

It should not be forgotten that implements and techniques for war and defence were advancing in Europe long before the Mount Hekla eruption. There is evidence from such sites as Haughey's Fort, which was probably erected after a period of warfare. Several archaeologists have suggested that the use of a ritual pond, such as that at the King's Stables, may have been an attempt by pagan Ulstermen to propitiate their water gods.

Many changes were taking place in Europe by the twelfth century BC, and they soon became evident in Ireland. Many sophisticated castings had been made by the use of clay moulds rather than the earlier stone moulds, which dropped out of use. With clay it is much easier to form different shapes and cast decorations. An object could be fashioned in wood and the wooden form could be pressed into clay to make a mould. In 1911 some wooden forms of bronze implements were recovered from a bog near the village of Tobermore, County Londonderry. As well as clay moulds, lead was sometimes added to the bronze to improve casting by retarding the speed at which the molten metal hardened. A whole new industry grew up that specialized in beaten bronze. This was developed to make large objects like bracelets, cauldrons and shields. As gold became abundant, Ulster goldsmiths made a great quantity of ornaments, not only for people in Ireland but also for export to the Continent.

Bronze and gold objects are not usually uncovered by archaeologists in the process of excavating sites. They are more often discovered by chance, as they have been along the River Bann. Sometimes they are discovered grouped together in a hoard of two or more metal objects. It is sometimes possible to approximate the date of an object by looking at the items found with it.

At Crevilly Valley, County Antrim, a hoard contained one axe and a chisel; at Clastry, County Down, a hoard also included a chisel. The objects appeared to be associated with woodworking, so it can be conjectured that they were part of a carpenter's tool kit. For some reason they were either lost or hidden in the ground. At Killymoon, County Tyrone, a hoard included a gold dress fastener. It had been inside a wooden box, and it was obviously a precious object, perhaps belonging to a wealthy member of the community. But why was it buried? People hid their precious objects in times of adversity. In later centuries, during the Viking invasions – not only of Ulster, but of the rest of Ireland – many hoards were hidden in bogs, and they are still being recovered today, from time to time. In Scandinavia a similar situation arose. Another theory is that the objects were offerings to the gods.

A bog near Dundrum, County Down, has produced a hoard with three spearheads, three axes, three rings and a pin. In some cases the objects seem to have been broken. Some hoards contain the kind of tools and scraps of metal we might expect to find in a foundry, and this has given rise to the term 'founder's hoard'. There appear to have been travelling smiths, but we do not yet understand why their belongings are so often found buried in the ground.

An advance in metallurgy took place in Ulster during the later Bronze Age. The Bishopsland phase, named after a hoard found in Bishopsland, Kildare, has been dated to between 1200 BC and 1000 BC. It includes a number of new woodworking tools, such as a hammer, a saw, a punch, a graver and a chisel. There are also 'ornament horizons' objects of gold: bracelets, necklets, hair clips and earrings. The little known Roscommon phase dating from 1000 BC, saw the introduction of the first swords. By about 900 BC the late Bronze Age is in full swing. The Dowris phase is named after a gigantic hoard recovered from Dowris, County Offaly. During this phase we find progressive developments in swords, and the introduction of bracelets, cauldrons, horns and shields.

Let us take a look at the weapons of the warrior, the ornaments of the wealthy, and the tools of the craftsmen.

During the middle Bronze Age an Ulster warrior was fitted out with a dirk or rapier and a spear. A revolution in ornaments and warfare swept across Europe and, at last, in about 1000 BC, reached Ireland. The sword was introduced. This heavy-bladed weapon was not used for thrusting like a rapier; it was used for slashing. The blade was extended from a full metal handle, which was covered with wool, bone or ivory, to form a hilt the warrior could grip firmly. The sword may have been carried in a scabbard fashioned out of some perishable material. A number of bronze swords have been found throughout Ulster, but the majority of finds come from the River Bann and Lough Erne.

In the late Bronze Age, riveting was introduced for fastening spearheads to shafts. As in the middle Bronze Age, the spearheads varied a lot, and it is likely that some were used as javelins and others in hand-to-hand combat.

Outside Ulster, bronze, wooden and leather shields have been uncovered from the late Bronze Age. A bronze shield might have been more fashionable than a leather shield, but it did not provide better protection. John Coles compared leather shields with bronze shields and he found that the point of a Bronze Age sword would run through bronze; a slashing blow could cut right into the metal. A leather shield, on the other hand, was able to deflect a severe sword blow. The shields were round and measured about 50 to 70 cm across. No shields have been found in Ulster, but a shield mould, made of alder, was found at Kilmahamogue, County Antrim. It is about 55 cm across, and it was used as a form to work leather into the shape of a shield.

The bow and arrow seem to have disappeared at this time. Barbed and fangled arrowheads were very plentiful in the early Bronze Age, but they seem to have disappeared by the late Bronze Age. They do not reappear until the time of the Vikings. It is not known why they disappeared.

How did important people in Ulster dress during the later Bronze Age? Not much is known about the dress of the early tribesmen in the province. Bronze and gold ornaments have been found, but they were confined to the richer inhabitants. The upper classes in the Ulster of the later Bronze Age may well have shaved their beards. A double-edged razor called a bifid (Latin *bifidus* 'split in two') is found in many places across Western Europe dating from this time. It seems that clean-shaven men in Ulster were fashionable.

Bronze Age clothing has not survived, and it is difficult to speculate upon what sort of clothes were worn. A piece of cloth has been recovered from Armoy, County Antrim. A small hoard of bronze objects, consisting of a socketed axe, a pin and a razor, were discovered in a peat bog, well wrapped in a woollen cloth with a tassel made out of horsehair. Cloth was woven, like that found sometimes in Bronze Age sites in Denmark, where items of clothing have been well preserved in burials. It is difficult to say whether a Bronze Age Ulsterman dressed in a similar fashion to a Bronze Age Dane. From evidence of how people elsewhere in North-West Europe dressed, it is possible that the piece of cloth from Armoy served as a type of belt. Clues about Bronze Age dress may also be gleaned from the ornaments that were fastened to them.

The most impressive objects from the late Bronze Age in Ulster are the gold ornaments. They suggest that Ireland was very rich in gold during this period. The ornaments took a variety of forms and a large number of them have been found in hoards. For example, fifteen simple penannular gold ornaments were discovered at Cathedral Hill, Downpatrick, County Down. Twisted ribbons and traces of gold have been uncovered in large numbers from the Inishowen and Largateany hoards in County Donegal. Items include dress and sleeve fasteners. The dress fastener is larger than the sleeve fastener. Archaeologists think that it was worn on an outer cloak. Exceptional finds like these have been uncovered from a bog in Lattoon, County Cavan, and they also include a beautifully decorated disc of a type also found elsewhere in Ireland. Sleeve fasteners tend to be found along the southern borders of Ulster.

Another way of fastening a cloak was with a bronze pin. Large disc-headed or sunflower pins of bronze were found in a hoard from Deryhale, County Armagh. Small bronze rings, some too small to have served as finger rings, were found at Haughey's Fort. A hoard discovered at Seacon, County Antrim, contained twenty-four small rings out of a total of about forty or fifty.

Neck ornaments of various materials were imported into Ulster from as far away as Scandinavia. An impressive necklace found at Kurin Moss, County Londonderry, was composed of 421 beads.

It is difficult to know whether or not metal tools were the property of only the wealthier members of society. Perhaps a crop surplus provided richer people with the means to obtain gold ornaments.

The socketed axe is the main tool encountered by archaeologists. The various stages in its development have been pointed out, from flanges, wings, stop bars and palstaves. They often carried a small ring which could be used to further support the handle. These axes seem to have been used as tools for clearing forests as well as having a wide variety of other uses. The socketed axe may have been the main tool assisting man in expanding agriculture production.

Some have suggested that the axe also served as a weapon. Many of the late Bronze Age axes were lightweight, and for forest-clearing they would have been inferior to the early and middle Bronze Age axes. Axes of many sizes were required in the late Bronze Age, not only to clear the landscape but also to serve in an increasingly sophisticated woodworking industry.

Axes have been found with other carpenters' tools, and this supports the view that some axes were tools rather than weapons. The discovery of chisels, awls, gouges, saws, hammers and knives shows that a new technology was at work in society. New bronze tools make it easier for craftsmen to work with wood. We have already seen some evidence for this in the dugout canoes and wooden vessels from Lough Eskragh and the wooden shield mould from Kilmahamogue, County Antrim.

A further development in the late Bronze Age was the use of sheets of bronze to make objects such as buckets and cauldrons. The large buckets were probably containers for liquid. They may have belonged to wealthy members of society. They may have been used in some form of ritual. The cauldron, another expensive object, could have been used for preparing feasts. A good example, made from bronze plates riveted together, comes from Lisdromturk, County Monaghan.

Fine bronze craftsmanship can be seen on bronze trumpets or

horns. These horns appear to have been blown on the side of the mouth. It has been hard to obtain much information about these instruments. O'Duibhir has recently carried out some experiments and has shown that they really can play music. Also there are horns shaped like the didgeridoo of the Australian Aborigine. We often find both types of horn together, as they were in a hoard discovered in 1840 in Drumbest Bay, County Antrim. O'Duibhir has suggested that the two different types of horn were meant to be played together. Horns found in Ulster are decorated with incised ornaments, but those found in Munster are decorated with spikes. At this time Ulster had close links with Britain and Scandinavia, and the fact that a considerable number of items not found in Ulster have been found in Munster suggests that the inhabitants of Munster probably drew on other areas for their inspiration.

Bronze Age burials have provided us with a few facts, but in the whole of Ireland not more than four burials have been assigned to the late Bronze Age. Two of these occurred in Ulster. At Mullaghmore, County Down, an earth mound that covered the ring ditch has been excavated. Within the mound, the remains of at least four people were uncovered. They had been cremated. Fragments of pottery were discovered with the human remains. Another cremation had taken place in an upright position. The style of the pottery suggests that it came from the later Bronze Age. On the Ballybeen housing estate near Dundonald, County Down, the cremated remains of an individual had been simply placed in the ground. A small ring ditch had been dug around the burial site, and it was filled with ashes, perhaps from the cremation fire. A piece of burnt wood yielded a radiocarbon date of between 900 BC and 775 BC.

Standing stones and stone circles appear to have been erected before the later Bronze Age. There was the ritual pond of the King's Stables in the Navan complex, County Armagh, but there is lack of evidence for ritual burials.

As we have seen, there is evidence that metal items were deposited in bogs and rivers, and this is also true of the Middle Ages, where again there is a lack of evidence for burials. Nearly half of all Bronze Age swords in Ulster have been found in rivers or bogs, and the situation in Britain is similar. Several explanations for this have been suggested. The swords may have been thrown into the water in some form of ritual or warriors may have been buried in rivers with their swords and only the swords have survived. Another possibility is suggested in Dark Age literature. In the tales of Cúchulainn and the Norse sagas we find that fights between warriors were often fought at fords or islands within rivers. Swords dredged from the River Bann and the River Erne may be the remains of prehistoric duels. However, Bronze Age hoards, many without weapons, have been recovered from wet environments (mainly bogs) so it cannot be assumed that discoveries in bogs and rivers are due to armed conflicts.

The depositing of valuable objects, especially metal objects, in water has been linked to ritual practice in many European countries. In the early historical period we learn from Posidonius that the Celts living about Toulouse about 100 BC left valuable objects in sacred lakes. Colin Burgess has suggested that this practice can be traced to the Bronze Age in the first millennium BC. There are similar suggestions concerning the King's Stables, where offerings could have been made in response to the impact that Mount Hekla had on the Irish weather.

Richard Bradley has proposed that the display and consumption of wealth differed from one period to another and perhaps from one area to another. Perhaps surpluses of goods were destroyed or disposed of during rituals and burials. This took place in the middle and late Bronze Age, in bogs and rivers, in clandestine acts initiated by the owners. To us in modern times this seems like irrational behaviour and it is more likely that wealthy families used their surplus wealth for the good of the community. Perhaps, too, wealthy men offered valuable objects to the gods on behalf of the whole community, and this conduct may have been expected of late Bronze Age leaders.

The Bronze Age finally ended after about 600 BC, and a great wealth of weapons and other artefacts disappeared from archaeological records. It is not clear what had happened. The collapse may have been due to natural causes, such as deterioration of the climate, or it may have been brought about by over-exploitation of the land. Climate deterioration has been observed elsewhere in North-West Europe. Some Irish pollen evidence suggests that the collapse coincides with the decrease in agriculture. However, too much can be read into pollen counts from upland bogs, such as Lacken Bog, County Down. Both pastoral and arable farming were carried on, and perhaps they became increasingly intensified in the lowlands of the province. Valerie Hall of Queen's University Belfast has obtained a pollen count from Long Lough, County Down, which shows pastoral clearance throughout the late Bronze Age.

The invasion of a new people has been associated with the Bronze Age collapse, and this has given rise to new theories about the arrival of the Celts in Ireland. Before 600 BC new sword types appeared in the island – notably the Hallstatt sword, which takes its name from the site of a very important cultural development on the Continent. This development has been attributed to Celtic peoples. These swords, which were made of iron, mark the beginning of the Iron Age in Western Europe. They have been discovered in the British Isles, especially in the Thames Valley, Eastern Scotland and Ireland. In Ulster they are associated with the River Bann and other rivers, continuing the association between rivers and swords. Some have suggested that finds of Hallstatt swords mark the path of the Celtic chieftains as they passed through England and Scotland and into Ireland. In support of this argument, it is pointed out that these swords are not usually found with late Bronze Age goods, and this may indicate that the people who wielded those weapons were often from outside the native population. Fifty iron Hallstatt swords have been found in Ireland. They do not look like the weapons of other invading warriors. Most archaeologists are of the opinion that the new swords represent little more than a new technique. Over Britain and Ulster, they say, there were few movements of people.

Traditional Irish history ascribes the foundation of Ulster to Rudraighe of the Fir Bolg at some time around the early Bronze Age. In the Bronze Age several different cultural patterns existed throughout the island, and regional variations are noticeable within the province. Wrist bracers, possibly of Beaker origin, are mainly found in County Antrim (there are only occasional finds in the south of Ireland); stone circles are clustered mainly in central Ulster; collared urns are mainly found in the east; wedge tombs in Ulster are found primarily in the south and west. George Eogan has called attention to how certain types of cauldrons, buckets, horns, rings and sleeve fasteners are found almost exclusively in the north; lock rings, gorgets (large golden collars) and certain types of horn and bowl are mainly found in Munster. However, many finds are not exclusive to Ulster; many objects are the same in the north as in the south.

Chapter 6

The Foundation of Ulster

The astronomer Ptolemy, in the second century, prepared a gazetteer of all the known peoples in the world. He listed the names of rivers, promontories, peoples and towns. Against each entry he gave its position according to his method of recording latitudes and longitudes. He started his survey with the most westerly land known – the land of Ireland.

Ptolemy's gazetteer is one of the earliest documents about Ulster in the Iron Age. However, it is very difficult to read his map. He never visited Ireland, but prepared his maps in the library of Alexandria in Egypt. The gathering of information was a long-drawn-out process, and there were numerous mistakes. During the Iron Age, British and Continental merchants traded with Ireland, and they gained some information about the geography of the island as they sailed along the coast and up the main rivers. This information was passed on to the Romans, who had almost conquered Britain in the first century AD. The Romans passed this information back to Rome and other centres of learning, such as libraries where Greek was spoken. From this it is possible to learn the original names of peoples and places in Ireland as they were conveyed by those who spoke the ancient British languages. They were written in Latin and Greek (Ptolemy's book was in Greek). There is no manuscript dating from Ptolemy's time, as the library at Alexandria was burned down in 642 AD. Therefore we depend on medieval copies.

The names on Ptolemy's maps are hard to decipher. They are often very different from the placenames as they appear today. On the Antrim/Down coast Ptolemy's map shows that a river known as the Logia emptied into the sea. From medieval manuscripts it is known that Belfast Harbour was called Loch Laoigh, ('the lough of the calf'). On Ptolemy's map the River Buvinda ('the white cow') is shown; today it is known as the River Boyne. Ptolemy calls Rathlin Island, off the north coast of Antrim, Ricina; Rechrann is the Irish name for Rathlin. The Rivios is identified with the Roe. There are no solid linguistic connections between these names, but there are various linguistic arguments to connect the other rivers on the north coast – the Vidva and the Argita – with the rivers Foyle, Bann and Bush.

Ptolemy also gives the names of rivers in other parts of Ireland: In the south-west was the Erdina, which some, like Liam Cogan, have associated with the Erne (Julius Pokorny thinks not). To the north, in Donegal, Ptolemy locates the Vennicnii, identified as the Venicones of South-East Scotland. In County Antrim were the Robogdii and Julius Pokorny suggests that this name comes from the old Irish ro-bochti, which meant very poor. During the Iron Age the Antrim coast was settled by the impoverished descendants of Neolithic fishermen. Others believe the name was corrupted before Ptolemy's great map came into being. Thomas O'Reilly has suggested that the name was originally something like Redodios, which later emerged as Rathlin. Liam Cogan, on the other hand, has suggested that the original name was Gobordii (Old Irish *gobor* 'horse'). On the east side of the Dalriada kingdom were the Epidii, whose name means horseman. Liam Cogan suggests that the two tribes occupied earlier sites in Ulster and Scotland. O'Reilly suggested that the Darina of South Antrim and North Down had descended from Davios, a traditional ancestor of both the Dalriada and the Dal Fiatach, who occupied West Down.

The most important of Ptolemy's tribes seem to have occupied Louth, South Down and Armagh. The Celtic name for the tribe was the 'Uluti' (Old Irish *Ulaid* 'Ulsterman'). The whole province

89

derives its name from the Uluti tribe, which occupied the north of Ireland by the second century AD.

In the annals of the Uluti there exists a place named Isamion. There is much debate amongst scholars as to what the word means. Linguists, such as Thomas O'Reilly and Julius Pokorny, argue that Ptolemy's Isamion was perhaps a version of Isamonis, which may have been shortened to Emain. Therefore Isamion may refer to Emain Macha, the ancient capital of Ulster. The Irish form of 'the' was put in front of Emain to give *an Ehmain* (pronounced 'uh-neven') and by the seventh century this passed into English as Navan. Another name for Ulster was Regia.

In the seventh and eighth centuries AD, Irish scholars started to compile a history of the Ulster peoples, recording the great battles between Ulstermen and their traditional enemies, the people of Connaught. These recount the adventures of Cúchulainn, Conchobar (Conor) MacNessa, Fergus mac Róich (Roy) and, of course, Deirdre (of the sorrows). In these tales Emain Macha is identified as the great capital of Ulster, where King Conor had his court and where feasts were held in honour of his warriors. The youths of Ulster were organized into the *macrad*, a boys' brigade. They played an early form of hurley and learned the techniques of warfare. The severed heads of their enemies were displayed. Druid poets immortalized the glories of Ulster warriors and their ladies in verse. The Red Branch Knights of Emain Macha were Ulster's equivalent of King Arthur's Knights of the Round Table. The Emain Macha of historical literature has been identified with Navan Fort.

By the late Bronze Age a major complex of sites had started to develop at Navan Fort, and round houses and compounds that might well be from the Iron Age have been investigated there. By the first century BC it appears to have been the capital of the Uluti – the original Ulstermen.

Around 100 BC the inhabitants of Navan cleared away the round houses and compounds to build an enormous circular structure. It measured about 40 metres across and was built in 275 parts arranged in six concentric rings. At the centre of the structure was a large piece of oak. This was raised on a ramp 6 metres long and built so that it might last for many centuries. It is difficult to determine exactly what the structure was like as today only the post-holes remain. Was the building roofed as some archaeologists suspect? Each post in the outer rings of posts was reinforced. As well as this, if the ramp for the central part was 6 metres long, it might be expected that the central piece of oak was roughly twice as long – that is, 12 metres. This central post seems to have been the last of the posts to be erected. This oak was dated by Mike Baillie of Queen's University Belfast, and the tree from which it came seems to have been cut down in 95 BC. The whole timber-built structure was at least 12 metres tall. It may have had a thatched roof, or it may have been open to the sky. Bernard Wailes has made a reconstruction showing what the building may have looked like: a timbered amphitheatre surrounding a series of free-standing parts with a 9-metre tower in the centre. Nothing was found in the floor of this great building, which appears to have been a large Celtic temple or hall. Perhaps it was like the one associated with the Red Branch Knights of Ulster folklore: nine compartments were in it, well built. Thirty feet was the height of each bronze front that was in the house. There were the remains of red yew within. The compartments of Conchobar were in the front of the house, displaying boards of silver with pillars of bronze. The King's headpiece glistened with gold and was set with jewels, with plates of silver above him to the rooftop of his house. The annals also record tales of the existence of a great palace, and the Ulster tales reflect the character of Iron Age times.

Near Navan Fort is Loughnashade, which today occupies less than a hectare and is only a shadow of its former self. In the Iron Age it was perhaps 2 hectares in extent; in prehistory it was 8 to 10 hectares. At the close of the eighteenth century men dug drains nearby and discovered remains, thought to be from the first century BC. They also discovered four great horns of the same age, which had been deposited in the lake as an offering. They are described as being in the traditional Celtic style. The great temple was still standing. Implements were made at Loughnashade ('the lake of the treasures') during the Iron Age. During excavation not only horns but also animal bones and some human skulls were discovered.

The 40-metre structure at Navan was probably made for ritual purposes, and perhaps it was ritually destroyed – probably during the first century BC. They filled the inside with limestone boulders to a height of over 2 metres. Dudley Waterman examined this stone cairn and he discovered that the people had set the outer wall on fire, but they did not touch the cairn. A lot of soil covered the structure to form an earth mound, which today is an impressive sight.

It is difficult to say why the structure was destroyed. It seems to have been a planned effort, perhaps by the local inhabitants. It is hard to imagine why the Uluti would destroy the temple, but the whole affair appears to have been accompanied by ceremony. It is conceivable that the building was destroyed as part of the funeral of a king. Another theory is that the temple itself was being sent into the next world. Traditionally, the other world was entered through a large mound. In the early Christian period Irish kings were inaugurated on mounds which were subsequently destroyed. After the temple was destroyed, Navan continued to serve as the site where the Kings of Ulster were crowned.

Navan Fort has been immortalized by historians and poets, but the record of other Iron Age settlements in Ulster is poor. However, we know from radiocarbon dating that a lot of Iron Age activity went on at Clogher, the other royal site, in County Tyrone. Iron Age artefacts were also found at Lyles Hill. Excavations at one of the huts on Scrabo Hill in County Down revealed Iron Age charcoal, and pit and a hearth at Mount Sandel, County Londonderry, were also dated to the Iron Age. Other Iron Age hearths were found at Bay Farm in Carnlough, and White Rock, both in County Antrim. There are Iron Age remains at Ballymulholland at Magilligan Strand, County Londonderry.

Along the southern border of ancient Ulster there are a series of earthworks that bear such names as the Dorsey, the Dane's Cast and, the most famous of all, Black Pig's Dyke.

The first of these, the Dorsey, is in South Armagh. It takes its name from the Irish *doicse*, and it has been regarded as a gateway into Ulster. The old coach road between Dublin and Armagh ran through the Dorsey. Here there is an enormous enclosure measuring about 4 km. A series of banks, a ditch and a timber palisade served for defence, but the purpose of the enclosure remains a mystery. Some archaeologists suggest that it was an enormous cattle enclosure. Chris Lynn has suggested that it might not have been an enclosure at all, but two lines of defensive earthworks built in different periods. They only appear to be joined up because the second earthwork was needed to plug the same hole as the first. Mike Baillie has uncovered some corroboration for this. Dendrochronology indicates that the northern earthwork was built about 150 BC and, as Lynn suspected, the southern line of defence was constructed about fifty years later, around 95 BC. Lynn draws our attention to evidence of burials along the northern palisade. The bodies may have been casualties of attacks on the palisade. The Dane's Cast remains undated. The Lisnadill Dane's Cast may have been a second or third line of defence for Emain Macha. The Clanrye Dane's Cast, on the other hand, runs north to south and along the border country of the greatly reduced territories of the Uluti after the demise of Emain Macha. This is considered to have been a later defence, raised up by the Ulster people occupying Central Down around AD 500.

Black Pig's Dyke derives its name from folklore. A schoolteacher magician was tricked into turning himself into a black pig, and he was then hunted across the southern borders of Ulster, raising up the ground and leaving behind him the ditch and bank which can be seen today. The main remains of earthworks are in South Armagh, Monaghan and South Donegal. The most thoroughly investigated are the earthworks near Scotstown, County Monaghan, where Aidan Walsh of the Monaghan County Museum carried out a preliminary investigation. There are two earth banks and the remains of a timber palisade, which have been dated to between 400 BC and 100 BC.

It is not clear what the purpose of the earthworks was. They seem to be defensive, built to impede attackers from the south. They are not continuous across the entire southern borders of Ulster. Rather, they appear where the territory does not offer natural protection, such as among the lakes of Fermanagh or on the elevated ground of South Armagh. It is not likely that they served as a manned defence, like Hadrian's Wall or the Great Wall of China. They were perhaps used as an impediment to cattle raiders.

The early annals suggest that the main preoccupation of early Ulstermen was cattle-raiding, especially between Ulster and Connaught.

The Connachta are said to have had their capital at Cruachan, now called Rathcroghan, County Roscommon. King Ailill and Queen Maeve may be characters out of early Irish fiction, but a kingdom involved in cattle-raiding may have been a reality.

Relics of Iron Age ceremonies in Ulster are hard to come by, as there is little evidence even of settlement. The diet of the inhabitants of Navan Fort – a royal or ritual site – may hardly be typical of most Ulstermen. Ballymulholland, an Iron Age shell-midden in North Londonderry, is perhaps not typical either. It has yielded evidence for only a few cows, pigs and sheep. This is a period characterized by much cattle-raiding and it is interesting to note that the only substantial Iron Age farm remains in Ireland – Knockaulin, County Kildare – show that the cattle were only 107 to 115 cm tall.

Ireland was regarded as a farmers' paradise in the Iron Age. Pomponius Mela wrote about AD 43 that the fields in Ireland were nutritious and savoury, and that the cattle ate their fill at a particular time of the day. If they were not restrained, he said, they would become sick with overfeeding.

There seems to have been a collapse in agricultural methods at the close of the Bronze Age, but in the Iron Age agriculture gradually recovered. Cereal cultivation seems to have been stepped up in some areas.

Two thousand querns have been found in Ireland, many in Ulster. They are different from the earlier saddle querns, where the method was to rub a stone across the face of the quern. The upper stone was now rotated on the lower, which was a much more efficient method. Grain was also more efficiently harvested than before, and there was a rise in population throughout Ireland. Seamus Caulfield has conjectured that new rotary querns indicate a new population in the island, since they are also found in Scotland and Northern England.

A wooden comb has been recovered at Navan Fort, and it is

thought that it was used to comb wool from sheep. Combs like this one have been found around the Iron Age hill forts of Southern England, but all evidence points to the fact that sheep were of secondary importance in prehistoric Ireland. The combs may also have been used in grooming the men and women of Iron Age Ulster.

The existence of Iron Age field systems is confirmed by discoveries at Mullaboy, County Londonderry, under a blanket of peat.

The introduction of iron tools into Ireland is a major problem for those speculating on the history of Ulster. Elsewhere in Europe, by the first century BC iron had replaced bronze for the manufacture of tools. Bronze made an effective tool, and the copper and tin needed for its production were readily available, but iron was found to have many advantages. It could be more easily shaped into a great variety of tools and it was more plentiful than either copper or tin. However, the extraction of iron from iron ore required new technology, so its use did not suddenly sweep across from the Caucasus Mountains, where it was first discovered. Iron tools only gradually replaced bronze tools, and the earliest iron tools were simply crude copies of Bronze Age tools.

At Toome Bridge in County Antrim, scorched iron axes have been uncovered. These are in the same general pattern as earlier bronze axes. The iron was forged, rather than cast like bronze, and it was then beaten into the shape of a socketed axe. Artefacts of iron are scarce in Ireland, and when they are found they are usually not so well preserved as bronze.

Meals were probably boiled and simmered in a great cauldron, like the one recovered from Dunlane, County Cavan. A bronze cauldron from Ballymoney, County Antrim, also dates from the Iron Age. In County Monaghan, at Altartate Glebe, there are remains of another cauldron.

The most prized possession of a warrior in Ulster was his sword, and more than twenty Iron Age swords have been discovered in the island. They are all iron except for a few wooden ones. The longest blade measures only 46 cm. The short sword is typical of Ireland, in contrast with Southern Britain, where very large Iron Age swords have been discovered. The British and Irish swords are of a similar style. Iron Age swords have also been discovered at La Tène sites. This was the major style of the Celts during the Iron Age. The handles were made out of organic material, such as bone or wood. Solinus wrote about the swords in the first century. The hilts of the swords were decorated with engravings of sea animals. A sword discovered at Ballyshannon in County Donegal had a metal hilt. It is different from all other Irish swords, although remains of a similar sword have been found in France. Archaeologists suspect that the Ballyshannon sword was imported into Ireland about the first century BC.

As well as swords, the remains of scabbards have been discovered – particularly the metal end piece. The most famous find of this kind was at Lisnacrogher, County Antrim, where a collection of scabbards and Iron Age weapons was discovered. Another major find was at the River Bann, where the scabbards are covered in decorations comparable to those of La Tène objects found in Britain and on the Continent (notably Central Europe). The warriors who used these expensive weapons must have been of a high social class. So many swords and scabbards have been found in County Antrim that archaeologists have suggested that there was an armoury there in the Iron Age.

The basic weapon of the warrior was the spear, which was less expensive to manufacture than the sword, for it did not use so much metal and was easier to make. The old Gaelic name for a spear was *gaisced* (Old Irish *gae* 'spear' *sciati* 'shield'). There were ceremonies when a young man came of age. It is very difficult to distinguish between a spearhead made in Ulster in the Iron Age and one made in a later period, but an elegant Iron Age spearhead was discovered at Boho, County Fermanagh. It is well decorated, as is a large spearhead found at Lisnacrogher, County Antrim.

There is an abundance of Iron Age spear butts. Sixty-one of them have been found in Ireland. They are generally regarded as serving to protect the end of the spear or to provide it with better balance. Several of these have been found attached to the remains of spear shafts. Spearheads were finished individually. Some are long and others resemble doorknobs. It has been suggested that they were not so much for warfare as for public demonstrations and other non-military purposes.

Only two Iron Age shields have been discovered in Ireland, and one of these was at Navan Fort. Others have been found in Britain. The Bronze Age warrior had a shield of oval or rectangular shape, and perhaps there was a small metal boss in the centre of the shield.

There is no specific Iron Age evidence for chariots in Ireland, but there is ample evidence for them in Britain. About one-quarter of all La Tène objects known in Ireland are earlier Bronze Age objects, but they include what seem to be pendants for horses.

A few of these have been found in pairs. They may have belonged to the upper classes, and, as Martyn Jope has observed, they may not be evidence of two-horse chariots. A mysterious 'Y' is associated with them. Wooden yokes have also been discovered in a bog near Dungannon, County Tyrone, similar to yokes discovered at La Tène sites on the Continent, but there is no evidence that they were used for chariots. The yoke could have been used for horses or cattle. Over 140 terrets (devices for holding the reins of chariots) have been found in Britain, but only one has been discovered in County Antrim, and that seems to have been imported from Scotland or Northern England. This perhaps suggests that Iron Age Ulstermen didn't use chariots to the extent that they were used in Britain, if at all. It is more likely that Ulster warriors used a small cart. The roads were perhaps worse in Ulster, where, for instance, there is no evidence of wooden trackways through boggy areas.

There is evidence of bog burials in Ireland, but only one (from Galway) during the Iron Age. Evidence of how people dressed comes almost exclusively from metal ornaments and other accessory items. The latter includes such articles as mirrors. The remains of the handle of a mirror were found at Ballybogey, County Antrim, decorated in the La Tène style. Other items have been discovered in the Donaghadee area in County Down.

The most common ornament to come down to us from the Iron Age is the fibula – a large brooch or clasp – which was used to fasten clothes together. It also served as an ornament. It is perhaps strange that archaeologists specialising in the Iron Age should not have recovered more evidence of fashions in pre-Christian Ulster.

Iron Age people would have wanted to wear the latest brooch or cloak or carry the latest shield. Many fibulae have been found on the Continent, but only twenty-five examples have been found in Ireland. Almost all of these were manufactured locally and used native elements of design.

There are three types of fibula: the simple fibula, the bow fibula, and the entirely Irish new-type fibula. Bow fibula can be divided into rod-bow and the broader leaf-bow fibulae. New-type fibulae have an ingenious design, and they have been uncovered in the area of Navan. Fibulae are almost always chance finds, except the leaf-bow fibulae recovered from an Iron Age grave at Kiltierney, County Fermanagh. Clothes were often fastened with the help of ring-heads, some of which were well decorated.

The most precious ornaments of the Iron Age are of gold, and these include bracelets and neck adornments. The most famous of these come from the great Broighter hoard, which was found near the River Roe in County Londonderry. It included two gold necklaces, a bowl and a small golden toy boat complete with oars. The Broighter hoard does not seem to have been the personal property of a single individual, but rather it is a collection of ornaments that may have been worn at a religious ceremony. Richard Warner has suggested that the hoard was deposited in water as an offering to a god, possibly the Gaelic sea god, Romnanan, who lived near to the Isle of Man. Bronze bracelets are also known.

Materials found at Newry, County Down, may have been imported from Scotland.

In the Iron Age, religion and art went together. It has been pointed out that the Broighter hoard may have been a religious offering. Another watery location, Loughnashade at Navan Fort, has yielded four bronze horns. At Ardbrin, County Down, two tablets were joined together with 1100 rivets to form an object measuring 1.4 m in length.

There is evidence that some wooden horns date from the Iron Age, and these have been found at Clogher, County Tyrone, and Diamond Hill at Killeshandra, County Cavan.

Iron Age metalwork has been divided into two main categories by Richard Warner, following on from the work of Martyn Jope of

Queen's University. The earliest art that he was able to date comes from the Iron Age I phase, and includes the decorated scabbards uncovered from Lisnacrogher. A series of S-shaped motifs are arranged symmetrically to fill the scabbard plates. The later Iron Age II phase is seen in the trumpets and oral bosses that have been found in the Broighter hoard and the River Bann disc, which is regarded as the greatest creation of Iron Age times in Ireland. This disc consists of a circular bronze plate about 10.5 m in diameter. It was made by tooling down the entire plate so that the design stood up in relief. There are three holes on its edge. Martyn Jope and Basil Wilson have suggested that it may have been worn on the breast or as the centrepiece of some form of headdress. This is not impossible, as comparable ornaments are associated with bronze headdresses, such as the Petrie Crown.

Not all Iron Age artefacts are of metal. Iron Age fashioned stones occur, though mainly outside Ulster. The Turoe Stone, from County Galway, is a well-known example. Other good examples have been found at Killycluggin, County Cavan, and Derrykeighan, County Antrim, where the ornament on the stone is similar to that on other Iron Age stonework. Barry Rafferty suggests that this stone dates to about the first century BC or AD. The Killycluggin Stone was perhaps associated with the pagan deity, and it may have been converted to service by Christian missionaries at a much later date. The Derrykeighan Stone was discovered in a gable wall of a ruined church.

The most graphic ornaments of pagan Ulster come in the form of stone and wood figures. A stone figure from a classic pagan cist at Corleck, County Cavan, has three heads. There are parallels across Western Europe that suggest that Corleck might have been the site of a shrine of a god. A stone head from County Cavan also belongs to the Iron Age, as perhaps does a wooden figure found at Ralaghan, County Cavan. The figure is complete, and it is thought to have been part of a fertility cult. To the north, another figure was found at Boa Island. A stone head from Beltany, County Donegal, may date from the Iron Age. The so-called Tandragee Idol, probably found near Newry, is now concealed in the vestry of St Patrick's Church (of Ireland) at Armagh. It is in the form of a helmeted soldier with another figure gripping his shoulder.

The fine metalwork of the Broighter hoard, the Loughnashade trumpets and great quantities of artefacts from the River Bann all indicate that offerings were made in rivers, lakes and bogs. Some may have been votive offerings. Martyn Jope suggests that bands of warriors dwelt near the rivers and they wore elaborate ornaments. There is also a hint that early ritual structures existed, like those associated with the Killycluggin Stone and the Beltany Head in the early Bronze Age.

There are not many remains of Iron Age burials in Ireland, but there is no reason to disbelieve the observations of the first century geographer Strabo that the Gaels honoured the descendants of their fathers. Only three Iron Age burials have been confirmed in Ulster. There were burials in the Iron Age ring barrows in the north of the island, but they may date from other periods.

At Dunadry near Antrim town, a large entrance mound, now destroyed, covered a stone cist in which a body had been laid out. Some ornaments accompanied the burial, including bracelets of glass and jet, but all of them have since been lost. Such ornaments are regarded as typical of Iron Age burials.

Kiltierney in County Fermanagh is the only Iron Age cemetery in Ulster. During the Iron Age a ditch was dug around a Neolithic passage tomb, and nineteen small mounds were erected on the outer edge of the ditch. A number of excavations have been carried out on the site, and evidence of Iron Age burials was discovered. Cremated bodies had been deposited into the earlier mound and the outer edge of the ditch, where they were covered in small mounds. Grave goods and perhaps clothes were included within the graves. Bronze Age brooches, glass beads and a bronze mirror were uncovered, but the evidence suggests that the burial took place around the first century BC.

There have been attempts to define Ulster as a separate entity before the Iron Age, but the material culture found in Ulster also extended outside its borders, and regional differences within Ulster were as sharply defined as those between Ulster and other parts of Ireland. The entire island was not culturally unified. Different tribes or clans fared better than others with the traditional division of

Ireland into Conn's half and Mug's half.

There are hints of political boundaries during the Iron Age, and these can be seen in royal capitals such as Navan Fort and Clogher and other linear earthworks. Defences erected along Ulster's borders during the Iron Age suggest the development of a political frontier that separated Ulster from the rest of Ireland. It is not known whether at this time there was a unified Ulster or not. There is every reason to be cautious about the numerous tales of the King of Emain Macha, who could command his forces from Downpatrick to the lakes of Erne and as far away as Dunseverick on the North Antrim coast. Ptolemy indicates the tribes occupying positions corresponding to the counties of modern Ulster. It is not certain whether or not power was exercised over the rest of Ulster from Emain Macha.

A political frontier may have developed between the fourth and first centuries BC in a line from Black Pig's Dyke and the Dorsey. La Tène metalwork in Ireland has been found not only in Ulster but also in Connaught and North Leinster. Only in Munster and South Leinster are La Tène objects seldom found. Some styles, such as Knockaulin, are only found north of the border (mostly at Lisnacrogher); other styles are found only at Black Pig's Dyke. Nevertheless, it is difficult to argue that there were major cultural differences between the north and south. It is possible to compare the structures at Navan with those at Knockaulin, County Kildare, the capital of Leinster.

County Antrim appears to have continued as a metallurgy centre throughout the prehistory period, with an important workshop at Lisnacrogher, and regional differences may account for the fact that many ring-headed pins have survived here but virtually no fibulae. By contrast, fibulae are well known at Armagh and Navan Fort. At Antrim are found regional styles unknown anywhere else.

Barry Rafferty has sited two main regional groupings of material within Ulster, one in the Bann Valley and the other in South Central Ulster, from the area of Navan Fort to Clogher, and south into Cavan. The north-west and south-east are not merely represented by La Tène metalwork. There are many examples of beehive querns from Down, Tyrone and Londonderry, but regional traditions remained strong in the province right through the Iron Age.

The linear earthworks may have defined the southern political limits of a greater Ulster, as depicted in the Ulster tales; but if so, the situation was probably short-lived. Tradition states that about AD 331 or 332, or perhaps as late as AD 450, the last King of Emain Macha, Fergus Fogha, was slain at a battle in County Monaghan. The victors are remembered in the legend as the Three Collas. They are said to have burnt Emain Macha and driven the Ulstermen east of the Lower Bann and the River Newry. In the early known feats, 'Ulster' refers to the present-day counties of Antrim and Down. By the seventh and eighth centuries, Christians started to record the folk tales of Ulster's golden age, which was said to have existed during what is known today as the Iron Age.

Amongst the early stories of ancient Ulster are the tales of *The Ulster Cycle*. They derive their name from the fact that most of the tales concern one or more of the legendary heroes who had been held in great repute as warriors of the Ulster kingdom. The tales record the continual fighting that went on between the Uluti and men of Ireland, as the men of Connaught were known to their traditional enemies in Ulster. The most famous tale is 'The Cattle Raid of Cooley'. It describes the armies of the rest of Ireland, and tells how Queen Maeve involved Ulster in the pursuit of a great bull. During the raid they were held off single-handedly by Cúchulainn until Ulster could organize its troops and defeat Connaught in a final battle.

The historical reliability of these tales has often been commented upon. The early Ulster annals recorded the events of *The Ulster Cycle* to the first century AD, and the Irish venerated the heroes of these stories. Cúchulainn, Conchobar, Conall Cernach and Deirdre all lived in what the early Christians saw as the distant past, and what we know as the Iron Age. The descriptions of the Ulster warriors accord satisfactorily with our knowledge of the early Celts. However, the Ulster heroes fought on chariots – a means of warfare that had not come to Ireland from the Celts on the Continent by the first century AD.

When a warrior was killed an enemy cut off his head and took it away as a trophy, and this practice was also known to the

Continental Celts. Ulster warriors boasted about their deeds and told tales of their champions, and this is described as a traditional Celtic custom in Gaul during the first century BC. Religious beliefs surrounded their tales. They looked to the Druids for fortune-telling and advice. In the tales the Ulster capital had fallen by the fifth century AD. After this, Ulster was limited to present-day Antrim, Down and North Louth. The Ulster tales have often been called a 'window into the Iron Age'.

Do the Ulster tales accurately describe life in Iron Age Ulster? The objects and excavations do not corroborate them to the extent some people have suggested. Cúchulainn regularly used a long sword that could cut people to bits or decapitate them, and swords were described as having gold hilts ornamented with silver and stones, but archaeologists have only found small Iron Age swords. They could hardly have had the devastating effects described in the Ulster tales. Apart from the metal hilt on the imported sword found at Ballyshannon, County Donegal, the hilts of Iron Age swords appear to have been made out of wood and bone. If we compare the swords described in the annals with those of the early Christian period and the Viking age, we often find similarities.

Despite detailed descriptions of the Ulster warriors in the tales we nowhere find descriptions of their spear hilts; therefore we cannot compare them with the great abundance of Iron Age spears that has survived in Ireland. We are told that their spears had silver binding rings, but this is not backed up by archaeological evidence. Silver was not employed in such a way until the early Christian period.

Descriptions of metal objects in the Ulster tales fit well with what we know of Irish metallurgy in the period between the seventh and tenth centuries. This is the period in which the tales were written down, so we can imagine that, although the early Irish writers may have taken the tales from ancient sources, they dressed the ancient heroes in the clothes and weapons of their early Christian contemporaries. We have almost no idea how Iron Age man dressed.

A lot of evidence of life in early Ulster comes from Emain Macha, the ancient capital, though much of it is not from the period when it was at its peak – in the first century BC. Long before the seventh century, Emain Macha became the site of a large grassy mound, and not the large circular structure of wood that obtained in the Iron Age, so the early Christian writers had even less idea of what Emain Macha originally looked like than we have today.

There is little archaeological evidence from the Iron Age, so we must look to early Irish literature and traditions in the hope of learning more about life in Ireland during this period. However, the information that has come down to us from medieval monks can hardly be trusted to give us an accurate picture of Ulster's pagan past.

The evidence of book literature suggests that during the Iron Age (and probably earlier) the population was organized into tribes, each of which was known in Old Irish as a *tuáth*. The ruler of each tribe was a king or *rí*. The property of the *tuáth* seems to have been dependent to a considerable extent on the wealth of the king. The king was perhaps inaugurated during a ceremony that involved ritual marriage with a mare or sow. This tradition continued in Ulster until about the thirteenth century, when the Norman writer Gerardus records that in a remote part of Ulster (Donegal), amongst the Cenel Connaill, a certain tribe was wont to install a king over itself by excessive savagery and an abundance of ritual. A white mare was brought forward in a beastly fashion. After the mare was killed it was boiled in water. The king got into the broth and ate the flesh that was brought to him. The rule of law and the role of king was consecrated. This is similar to a ceremony carried out in Ireland by the ancient Celts. It was believed that the well-being of society depended on such rituals.

Medieval monks provide us with a considerable amount of information about the Druids.

'War-bands' (*cuire*) were made up of young males of the same age – perhaps fourteen years of age, when they were not yet married or settled down within the *tuáth*. They imitated the behaviour of wolves, and sometimes went into battle naked. They were ferocious in combat – the Irish equivalent of the Norse berserkers.

The assumption can be made that the people who occupied Ulster during the Iron Age spoke some form of Gaelic. Irish emerged as a linguistic entity – part of the Celtic group of languages. By the time of the earliest written documents, Irish is the only known language of ancient Ireland, north or south.

The earliest information about languages in Ireland is Ptolemy's gazetteer.

Fifty-five names are mentioned, and many of these have been recognized as Celtic. It cannot be proven with certainty that they are the actual Irish names or corruptions of those names.

On the Continent the main Celtic languages include Gaulish, the language of the tribes of Gaul that fought against Julius Caesar; Lepontic, a Celtic language spoken in northern Italy near Milan before the Romans established themselves in Italy; and Hispano-Celtic, the language of northern Spain and Portugal. In Britain there were two basic branches of the Celtic language: Goidelic and Brittonic. The Celts had occupied Britain before the Romans invaded. The Brittonic languages included Welsh, Cornish (now a dead language) and Breton, which came to Brittany about the time of the Anglo-Saxon conquest of Britain. The Goidelic languages include Irish, Scottish Gaelic and Manx (another dead language).

In Old Irish the Celtic 'Q' became a 'C', whereas in Brittonic languages the 'Q' had a 'P' sound. We now speak of 'Q' Celtic and 'P' Celtic. There are many differences between Irish and Welsh forms of Celtic.

Ptolemy's map of Ireland has names that were obviously Celtic, but they cannot be safely assigned to either Goidelic or Brittonic branches. There may have been British tribes in Ireland during the Iron Age, and this might explain the anomalies found in Ptolemy's gazetteer.

There are names that appear to be Brittonic of the 'P' Celtic type. A Leinster tribe was called the Manapii; in Irish it is more likely to have been styled the Managi or Manacii. It has been proposed by Thomas O'Reilly that Ireland was originally British (in a linguistic sense). O'Reilly has suggested that Ptolemy's map might have been drawn up using an older map, originally compiled by the Greek explorer Pytheas. Pytheas sailed around North-West Europe in the fourth century BC. Later, during the period 150 BC to 50 BC, according to O'Reilly, Celtic peoples speaking a language near to Irish crossed from the Continent to subdue Ireland.

However, O'Reilly suggests that this did not make much impact, and that by the first century AD the Goidelic and Brittonic languages were still very similar in pronunciation.

On the other hand, the presence of British tribes within Ireland cannot be discounted altogether. Both tradition and archaeological evidence indicate that the Laigan (who derived their name from Leinster) were British and Gaulish in origin. There were close contacts between Ulster and Scotland in the Iron Age, and there may have been considerable comings and goings between the two lands. This may have included a movement of British population into Ireland.

The remains of an Iron Age burial were discovered in about 1851 near a still unidentified place called 'Loughey' near Donaghadee, County Down. The burial site was discovered when systematic archaeological digs were still unknown in Ireland. The remains of a cremated woman had been placed in a small pit. A bronze fibula, tweezers, rings (and other bronze objects), several glass bracelets and about 150 glass beads were found at the same site. They seem to have come from Southern Britain about the first century AD. The woman may have belonged to a wealthy family and she was probably buried in accordance with the rites of her family. When Martyn Jope and Basil Wilson rediscovered the remains, they suggested that she might have been either a refugee from Southern Britain fleeing before the Roman invaders, or she had voyaged to Ireland on a merchant ship.

Ptolemy's map of Ireland seems to show that there were Celtic tribes in Ireland, but it is not known which version or versions of the Celtic language were spoken. The earliest examples of Irish do not occur until the erection of ogham stones in the fourth century. Ogham stones were erected to commemorate someone's death. The inscriptions on the stones commemorate people who had died and record their names. They are chiefly found in Munster, in the south-west of the island, but some are known in Ulster.

There is a strong similarity between the earliest known Celtic names and the names as recorded on Ptolemy's map. This fact, coupled with the evidence of the ogham stones, indicates that it is unlikely that the Celts had been in Ireland for a long time. If they had, there might by that time have been a greater difference between the languages spoken in Britain and Ireland. They had not been separated long enough for major linguistic divisions to have arisen. Colin Renfrew has attempted to push back the origins of the Irish language all the way to the Neolithic.

Evidence for migration during the period between about 1000 BC and 100 BC is slight. After about 700 BC we saw that foreign goods – such as swords of the Hallstatt style – started to appear in Ireland, but archaeologists have not been impressed by the idea of movement of people into the island at this time. On the other hand, they cannot totally exclude the possibility.

A second date for a possible wave of immigrants is about 300 BC, when we find the first La Tène artefacts in Ireland – especially in the north of the island. Here the evidence is more convincing; mainly associated with swords and scabbards, it seems to take its inspiration directly from central Europe – possibly from Northern France. Martyn Jope and Richard Warner, amongst others, have suggested that the appearance of La Tène objects, particularly swords and scabbards, shows that immigrants from Central Europe and possibly Northern France had crossed into Ulster. Most archaeologists remain unconvinced.

All of Ireland became Gaelic-speaking, not just Ulster.

At last, in about AD 100, another influx of La Tène material appeared in Ireland. Evidence is sparse, but it does not point to a planned invasion.

Perhaps Irish-speaking Celts first arrived in the island. Perhaps they arrived sometime before the fifth century, at a date when the ogham stones were erected. They seem linguistically more likely to have their roots in the first millennium BC than in a much earlier time.

By the end of the fifth century AD, Ulstermen started to colonize South-West Scotland to form the kingdom of Dalriada (named after Dál Riata) which spanned the northern part of the North Channel. The Gaelic language expanded inland and eventually embraced almost all of Scotland by about AD 1000. The colonization perhaps explains the origins of the Scottish Gaelic tongue. Prior to this the people of

Scotland spoke Brittonic or Pictish. This process may have taken place over nearly 600 years. There may have been short-term migration between Ireland and Britain, and perhaps also from Europe.

Irish colonists may have drifted into Ireland over the course of many generations during the first millennium BC, and gradually they assimilated the local population and spread their language through Ireland.

It is often thought that invaders swept into the country, brandishing their swords, so that soon everyone was speaking their language. People, however, do not give up their language easily. At first Irish seems to have been the language of the wealthier members of society, so this may have meant that the tribes became bilingual, just as today many Irish people speak Irish and English. Over a number of generations, the tribes must have given up their earlier language as more and more children were brought up to speak Irish. The early Irish had something to offer the main population of the island, and they gradually enticed them away from their native tongue. With the apparent collapse of the late Bronze Age society, as the old order passed away, batches of Irish speakers entered Ireland and the native population were gradually absorbed into Irish-speaking communities. If the newcomers occupied Navan Fort, they controlled a major ritual and trade centre. The native population may have learnt Irish so that they could participate in public rituals.

It is just possible that the Irish arrived during the late Bronze Age, when hill forts were established. If the architects of the hill forts had been Goidelic speakers, the local population may have been attracted to learning the new language in order to participate in the new aristocratic society and enjoy the protection and economic benefits it afforded. This is, of course, speculation.

In the period before the Gaelic occupation of Ireland, there were many invaders: the Cessair, Partholan, Fir Bolg, Tuatha Dé Danann and the Sons of Mill. The mixing of Irish traditional astrology with archaeology produces a brew much too strong for the stomach. The early Irish are likened to a lost tribe in the island. Scholars like Thomas O'Reilly have examined the various myths that existed before the final establishment of the Irish in the island. Other attempts to separate the prehistoric wheat from mythological chaff have been carried out.

Early Irish tradition also mentions a number of ethnic groups, one of which was the Cruthin or Ancient Kindred. The Cruthin have received widespread attention in Ulster, since they are deemed to have been the original people of the island. The name 'Cruthin' is the Irish form of 'Priteni', from which the name 'Pretanic Isles' is derived – hence, British Isles. The Cruthin in Ulster were later assimilated by the Goidelic or Irish invaders, but it can be argued that the Cruthin returned from Scotland to reclaim their ancient roots during the plantation period. It is impossible to ignore the Cruthin presence for there is abundant evidence for them in the British Isles, presumably derived from Neolithic colonists. La Tène objects dating from the third century BC have been found. Warner has examined the early Iron Age II material, perhaps derived from Britain, which suggests that there was a Belgae (Fir Bolg) population.

From tribes such as the Uluti are descended the medieval peoples of Ireland. Ian Adamson says the Irish came from Spain about the second century AD and he says that, in the conquest of all Ireland, the Cruthin in the north held out the longest.

It is difficult to know whether or not the Cruthin formed a separate ethnic group. If the Ancient Kindred descended from the original Neolithic population of Ireland, perhaps a Scots-Irish identity may be in order. The late Mesolithic period appears to have been the last period where similarities throughout Ireland outweighed regional differences. It is doubtful that the population of Britain and Ireland saw themselves as a common people at any time since the Neolithic.

In Ulster the Cruthin were chiefly in County Antrim and parts of West Down – the land of the Dál Fiatach in the early Christian period. Here have been found remains akin to those of Northern Britain and Scotland, so it has been hard to find facts about a distinct Cruthin culture. There is a similarity between the Cruthin and the Picts of Northern Scotland. The Ulster Cruthin seem to represent a later colonization into parts of Ireland from Scotland by early pre-

Celtic or Celtic peoples. It is thought that they did not speak anything but Irish. The idea of an invasion of Celts from Spain in the second century has little archaeological support.

During the first century AD the Roman Empire conquered Britain – a process that had been started by Julius Caesar a century before. Ulster now had hostile neighbours, but the Romans had little information about their poor next-door neighbours. The first-century geographer Strabo tells us that the natives were highly savage, and that Ireland represented the limits of the inhabited world. Solinus, in the third century, mentions the legend that St Patrick chased all the snakes out of the island. The Irish tribes were said to be inhospitable and warlike: they drank a lot, and Irish warriors smeared the blood of their dead enemies across their faces. Solinus also mentions the difficult sea crossing from Britain into Ireland, and he says that the natives sailed in boats of wickerwork covered in ox hides.

Agricola, the Roman governor of Britain, was responsible for conquering Northern Britain, and his son-in-law, Tacitus, wrote a short biography of his father-in-law. Tacitus tells how the Romans, after subjecting Britain, eventually turned their attention to Ireland. He mentions the soil and climate, and says that its population, differed little from that of Britain. Ireland had good harbours, and it was said that a few legions could conquer and occupy the island.

The most spectacular evidence for contact between Ulster and Britain at this time is a hoard of 150 silver coins found in the ground at Ballinrees, County Londonderry. As well as the coins, there were two spears and over 400 ounces of silver plates and bowls. Another treasure was uncovered by a farmer, James Quig. He was digging potatoes in 1831 at Feigh Mountain, County Antrim. When he lifted a stone he found 500 silver coins. Other sites have yielded other Roman items, such as Romano-British brooches discovered in sand dunes at Ballyness and Dunfanaghy, County Donegal.

Roman artefacts are occasionally found in Ulster sites such as amphitheatres. A Roman water jug was found at Clogher, County Tyrone. These finds confirm that there was contact between Ireland and Roman Britain. In some cases, however, the objects may have been the spoils of piracy; Irish pirates raided the coast of Roman

Britain and captured Roman merchant ships. During the Roman occupation, too, it is thought that large numbers of people may have come to Ireland to escape the tyranny of the invaders.

During the second century AD there were continual contacts between Roman Britain and Ireland, in the form of trade and refugees. At this time the Romans feared that the Irish, particularly the Scotti of Ulster, might try to conquer Britain. By the fourth century the Irish were colonizing Wales, the Isle of Man and the western coast of Scotland. Cemeteries have been discovered as well as Romano-British fashions in dress, ornaments and weaponry. A weaving industry started to make its appearance in the island. Perhaps at this time the ogham script was developed.

By the mid-fifth century AD Christianity had come to Ulster, and this brings our study of pre-Christian Ulster to an end.

Select Bibliography

Des Lavelle, *Skellig: Island Outpost of Europe* (The O'Brien Press, 1976).

Ernest Sandford, *Discover Northern Ireland* (Northern Ireland Tourist Board, 1981).

Henry Boylan, *The Boyne: A Valley of Kings* (The O'Brien Press, 1988).

Iain Zaczek, *The Book of Irish Legends* (Cico Books, 2001).

J. D. C. Marshall, *Dalriada: A Guide round the Celtic Kingdom* (Glenariff Development Group, 1998).

J. P. Mallory and T. E. McNeill, *The Archaeology of Ulster from Colonization to Plantation* (The Institute of Irish Studies, 1995).

Noreen Cunningham and Pat McGinn, *The Gap of the North* (The O'Brien Press, 2001).

N. L. Thomas, *Irish Symbols of 3500 BC* (Mercier Press, 1998).

Patrick Heraughty, *Inishmurray: Ancient Monastic Island* (The O'Brien Press, 1982).

Patrick J. McKeever, *A Story Through Time* (Geological Survey of Ireland, 1999).

Robert Macalister, *The Archaeology of Ireland* (Bracken Books, 1996).

Sean Connors, *Mapping Ireland: From Kingdoms to Counties* (Mercier Press, 1976).